Performativity, Politics and Education

Educational Futures

RETHINKING THEORY AND PRACTICE

Series Editor

Michael A. Peters (*Beijing Normal University, P.R. China*)

Editorial Board

Michael Apple (*University of Wisconsin-Madison, USA*)
Tina Besley (*Beijing Normal University, P.R. China*)
Gert Biesta (*University of Edinburgh, UK*)
Liz Jackson (*Educational University of Hong Kong, Hong Kong*)
Jian Li (*Beijing Normal University, P.R. China*)
Gary McCulloch (*London Institute of Education, UK*)
Mark Olssen (*University of Surrey, UK*)
Fazal Rizvi (*University of Melbourne, Australia*)
Susan Robertson (*University of Cambridge, UK*)
Linda Tuhiwai Smith (*University of Waikato, New Zealand*)
Arun Kumar Tripathi (*Indian Institute of Technology, Mandi, Himachal Pradesh, India*)
Eryong Xue (*Beijing Normal University, P.R. China*)

VOLUME 76

The titles published in this series are listed at *brill.com/edfu*

Performativity, Politics and Education

From Policy to Philosophy

By

Peter Roberts

BRILL

LEIDEN | BOSTON

All chapters in this book have undergone peer review.

The Library of Congress Cataloging-in-Publication Data is available online at https://catalog.loc.gov

Typeface for the Latin, Greek, and Cyrillic scripts: "Brill". See and download: brill.com/brill-typeface.

ISSN 2214-9864
ISBN 978-90-04-51815-5 (paperback)
ISBN 978-90-04-51816-2 (hardback)
ISBN 978-90-04-51817-9 (e-book)

Copyright 2022 by Koninklijke Brill NV, Leiden, The Netherlands, except where stated otherwise. Koninklijke Brill NV incorporates the imprints Brill, Brill Nijhoff, Brill Hotei, Brill Schöningh, Brill Fink, Brill mentis, Vandenhoeck & Ruprecht, Böhlau and V&R unipress.
All rights reserved. No part of this publication may be reproduced, translated, stored in a retrieval system, or transmitted in any form or by any means, electronic, mechanical, photocopying, recording or otherwise, without prior written permission from the publisher. Requests for re-use and/or translations must be addressed to Koninklijke Brill NV via brill.com or copyright.com.

This book is printed on acid-free paper and produced in a sustainable manner.

Contents

Notes on Original Publications   VII

Introduction: From Policy to Philosophy: Education in the Era of Performativity   1

1 **Performativity, Big Data and Higher Education: The Death of the Professor?**   8
   1   Introduction   8
   2   Knowledge, Performativity and the Death of the Professor   8
   3   Higher Education in the Age of Big Data   12
   4   Conclusion   21

2 **Academic Dystopia: Knowledge, Efficiency and Intellectual Life**   23
   1   Introduction   23
   2   Knowledge, Efficiency and Performativity   24
   3   Performance-Based Research Funding in New Zealand   26
   4   Lyotard, Tertiary Education and the PBRF   29
   5   Conclusion: A Dystopian Future for the Academy?   37

3 **Higher Education, Impact and the Internet: Publishing, Politics and Performativity**   42
   1   Introduction   42
   2   Scholarly Publishing in the Age of the Internet   42
   3   Peer Review, Performativity and Impact   45
   4   Concluding Remarks   53

4 **Problematising Productivity: Neoliberalism, Wellbeing and Education**   55
   1   Introduction   55
   2   The Productivity Commission's Report: Context and Content   56
   3   A Critique   62
   4   Conclusion   72

5 **'It Was the Best of Times, It Was the Worst of Times …': Philosophy of Education in the Contemporary World**   74
   1   Introduction   74
   2   Shifting Sands: The Evolution of PESA   74

VI   CONTENTS

   3   Philosophy of Education as a Way of Life   81
   4   Conclusion   87

6   A Philosophy of Hope: Pedagogy, Politics and Humanisation   88
   1   Introduction   88
   2   Paulo Freire: Philosophy, Pedagogy, Practice   91
   3   Critical, Engaged Teaching: Ira Shor and bell hooks   97
   4   Conclusion: A Philosophy of Hope   101

7   Philosophy of Education as a Way of Life: A Case Study   105
   1   Introduction   105
   2   Schooling and University Experiences   105
   3   Academic Life   110
   4   Conclusion   118

References   121
Index   145

Notes on Original Publications

The author and publisher gratefully acknowledge permission to reproduce material from the following sources:

Chapter 1 first appeared as Roberts, P. (2019). Performativity, big data and higher education: The death of the professor? *Beijing International Review of Education, 1*(1), 73–91. With permission from Brill (https://brill.com).

The original version of Chapter 2 was published as Roberts, P. (2013). Academic dystopia: Knowledge, performativity and tertiary education. *The Review of Education, Pedagogy, and Cultural Studies, 35*(1), 27–43. By permission of the publisher (Taylor and Francis Group: www.tandfonline.com).

Chapter 3 is based on Roberts, P. (2019). Higher education, impact, and the Internet: Publishing, politics and performativity. *First Monday: The Peer-Reviewed Journal on the Internet, 24*(5). http://dx.doi.org/10.5210/fm.v24i5.9474. With permission from the Editor (https://firstmonday.org/).

Chapter 5 is a revised version of Roberts, P. (2013). 'It was the best of times, it was the worst of times ...': Philosophy of education in the contemporary world. *Studies in Philosophy and Education, 34*(6), 623–634. With kind permission from Springer Science+Business Media.

Chapter 6 was first published as Roberts, P. (2021). A philosophy of hope: Paulo Freire and critical pedagogy. In A. Pagès (Ed.), *A history of Western philosophy of education in the contemporary landscape* (pp. 107–128). Bloomsbury. With permission from Bloomsbury Academic, an imprint of Bloomsbury Publishing Plc. (https://www.bloomsbury.com/).

Chapter 7 is an updated version of Roberts, P. (2014). An accident waiting to happen: Reflections on a philosophical life in Education. In L. J. Waks (Ed.), *Leaders in philosophy of education* (Vol. 2, pp. 211–229). Sense Publishers. With permission from Brill (https://brill.com).

INTRODUCTION

From Policy to Philosophy

Education in the Era of Performativity

Among educationists with an interest in policy, it is not altogether uncommon to find a certain weariness being expressed when words such as 'neoliberalism', 'managerialism', 'commodification', and 'performativity' are uttered. Some scholars believe the moment for theorising policy changes in education in these terms has passed. They may claim that we live in a post-neoliberal era, distinguishing this from earlier stages in the development of free-market economies. Or, it might be suggested that the term 'neoliberalism' applies only to reform in the economic sphere and has no place in discussions of changes in social policy. For some academics, there is simply a desire to 'keep moving'; to constantly find new ways of understanding and addressing policy problems. Younger scholars may have known nothing but managerialism in their professional lives, and might wonder what all the fuss is about; for them, the university as experienced in the present day is 'business as usual', and appeals by older colleagues to different approaches in the past may seem empty, 'old-hat', or hopelessly romanticised. Terms such as 'performativity' have, others might argue, been overused and undertheorised. In some cases, references to knowledge being treated as a commodity can draw an indifferent shrug. 'So what?', it might said; '*of course* knowledge is "bought" and "sold" – that's how contemporary global capitalism works'.[1]

This weariness is, however, also a reflection of the dominance of neoliberal ideas in shaping policy agendas around the world. We are 'tired' of these ideas partly because they have seeped into so many aspects of our lives. We can detect their influence, even if only indirectly, in the way we work, communicate, travel, shop, eat, and entertain ourselves. It is certainly true that neoliberalism, as an implied philosophy underpinning government policy, has evolved and changed over time. Indeed, strictly speaking, there has never been a single, coherent doctrine, applied in the same ways in all contexts, called 'neoliberalism'. Neoliberalism always has been a hybrid, mixing elements of monetarism, transaction cost economics, human capital theory, agency theory, and public choice theory (Olssen, 2001). In some respects, it would be more appropriate to use the term only in the plural, as 'neoliberalisms', distinguishing, for example, 'Third Way' variants from the 'more market' approaches adopted in earlier years. But this is rather cumbersome, and it is possible to acknowledge

© KONINKLIJKE BRILL NV, LEIDEN, 2022 | DOI:10.1163/9789004518179_001

heterogeneity in the development and application of neoliberal ideas, while also recognising enduring themes and patterns in policy and practice.

In identifying thematic continuities, education at the tertiary level provides an especially interesting and revealing case study. In New Zealand, for example, despite shifts in emphasis with changes in government, there has over the last thirty years been a persistent tendency to treat higher education as a business, subject to the same laws of the market as other commercial activities. Competition within and between institutions has been encouraged; students have been regarded as perpetually choosing 'consumers'; and substantial sums of money have been devoted to 'branding' and marketing exercises. The need to 'perform' (in individual, institutional and international terms) has constantly been stressed. There has been a relentless drive to extract ever-greater efficiencies from the system, with the aim being to maximise quantifiable outputs relative to inputs. Academics have been encouraged to become more entrepreneurial in their activities, and those who undertake research in areas that attract significant funding from external bodies can be expect to be well rewarded by their institutions. The notion of the university serving a 'public good' role has largely disappeared from policy discourse (usually attracting, at most, only a few cursory comments) and in its place a view of students as self-interested, private beneficiaries of their educational investments has prevailed. Governance structures have also changed, with institutional leaders now being seen as the equivalent of chief executive officers, new divisions between 'management' and academic staff, and increasingly intrusive auditing, monitoring and reporting practices. Similar trends have been evident in Australia, the United Kingdom, Canada, the United States, and other parts of the world.

This book does not set out to provide a detailed theoretical examination of neoliberalism and managerialism; scholarship of that kind is readily available elsewhere.[2] Rather, it has a more applied focus on how performativity, as an expression of neoliberal and managerialist thinking, 'works' in specific policy contexts. It pays particular attention to the tertiary education sector and considers how the logic of performativity shapes and distorts notions of what it means to engage in worthwhile research, what it means to be 'well', and, ultimately, what it means to be human.[3] I argue that performativity, as exemplified by the practices associated with contemporary tertiary education and research policy, is dehumanising. The work of Jean-François Lyotard provides a helpful starting point in understanding how and why this is so. The ideas advanced in *The Postmodern Condition* (Lyotard, 1984), Lyotard's classic account of the application of the performativity principle in post-industrial, computerised societies, continue to resonate today. But as a concise 'report on knowledge', *The Postmodern Condition* also has its limits. Lyotard's references to dehumanisation are tantalisingly brief, and there are other thinkers who have given this concept much deeper thought. Perhaps the best known, in educational circles at least, is Paulo Freire, whose ideas also feature in this book. Freire, like Lyotard, has something distinctive to offer when responding to the neoliberal changes of recent decades. He is one among many theorists to whom we can turn in seeking humanising alternatives to the dominant policy paradigms of our age.

The progression in this book is 'from policy to philosophy', in two senses. First, this idea is reflected in the structure of the volume, with Chapters 1 to 4 devoted principally to policy themes and Chapters 5 to 7 having a stronger philosophical flavour. Second, and more importantly, a central underlying claim of the book is that philosophy gives us an 'answer' to the problem that is performativity. Note that this is *an* answer, not *the* answer. Philosophical work in education rubs against the logic of performativity. It fosters a critical orientation toward the world and a questioning of received educational wisdom. Philosophers of education have, over the last three decades, frequently addressed policy matters in their work. They have identified, analysed and evaluated the ontological, epistemological, ethical, and political assumptions underpinning neoliberal reforms. Philosophy of education is, however, not merely a domain of scholarly activity but a *way of life*. It implies a certain restlessness; a need to keep inquiring, keep probing, even if there is little certainty about where this will lead. In a world governed by the principle of performativity, the goals of efficiency, measurability and predictability are all important. A philosophical life in education is often unpredictable, uncertain and 'inefficient'. Those committed to living this way will value knowledge and education not just for the income they can generate but for their own sake. They may see merit in measuring some things while also stressing that much of what matters most in education, and in human life more generally, is *im*measurable.

Some of the obstacles in the way of taking immeasurability seriously, and of running counter to the prevailing discourse of performativity, are highlighted in Chapter 1. The educational reality we inhabit, this chapter points out, is one increasingly structured by 'big data'. We rely, more and more, on numbers, not only in measuring economic success but also in assessing our educational efforts. There has been a strong push to make education more 'scientific' via 'evidence-based' initiatives, and there is now an obsession with rankings and performance on international league tables. These developments, the chapter suggests, are not new but rather represent a continuation of trends already underway half a century ago. Lyotard (1984) could see that scientific knowledge, already in the ascendancy, would continue to dominate narrative knowledge. Knowledge would, he predicted, be seen as a commodity: as something to be bought and sold on international markets. More than this, though, Lyotard foresaw a grim future for those teaching in institutions of higher education. Advancements in technology, coupled with the commodification of knowledge and the dominance of the performativity principle, would, he believed, sound the knell of the age of the professor. This famous 'death of the professor' thesis serves as a focal point for the chapter, setting up the rest of the book. I argue that the age of the professor has not yet passed, but I accept that it is, in some respects, *dying*. The chapter identifies some of the key elements of this process of dying, pointing to the dehumanising nature of the changes currently occurring.

The stark realities of the present detailed in the first chapter find further elaboration in Chapter 2, where attention turns to a key area for the application of the performativity principle, namely, the assessment of research. Other ideas from Lyotard are explored here and found to have particular relevance for the New Zealand context. The primary means for determining government funding for tertiary education institutions and organisations in New Zealand is the Performance-Based Research Fund (PBRF). First introduced almost two decades ago, the PBRF has now cemented itself in institutional consciousness. It has left an indelible mark on research activities within institutions such as universities, shaping how researchers view themselves and the work they undertake in their fields of study. I point to the limiting language of 'outputs', the incentives for competition instead of collegiality, and the dehumanising character of machine-like production under the PBRF. I argue that these changes, collectively, constitute a kind of academic dystopia, signalling a need not for a nostalgic return to a romanticised past but for new critical utopian thinking among those working in the tertiary sector.

Chapter 3 considers how and why scholarly publishing has changed over the last two decades. It discusses the role of the Internet in overcoming earlier barriers to the rapid circulation of ideas and in opening up new forms of academic communication. While we live in a world increasingly dominated by images, the written word remains vital to academic life, and more published scholarly material is being produced than ever before. The chapter argues that the Internet provides only part of the explanation for this increase in the volume of written material; another key contributing factor is, as foreshadowed in Chapter 2, the use of performance-based research funding systems in assessing scholarly work. Having argued in Chapter 2 that such schemes can be dehumanising, I point out in Chapter 3 that it could be worse. Of even greater concern than the assessments carried out under regimes such as the PBRF are systems based largely or entirely on metrics, 'impact', and revenue generation. The chapter critiques these trends, makes a case for the continuing value of peer review, and comments briefly on the subversive potential of the Internet in resisting the dehumanisation of scholarly work.

Evidence for the claim that neoliberal ideas continue to leave their mark on policy thinking can be found in the work of New Zealand's Productivity Commission. A body formed to provide advice to government, the Productivity Commission has released a substantial report on tertiary education, with recommendations that owe much to the neoliberal reforms of the 1990s. The twin pillars of 'choice' and 'competition' are given particular emphasis. These ideas and others are advanced on the basis that they will enhance efficiency, productivity, prosperity, and wellbeing. The reference to wellbeing is of particular interest, for this reflects a broader shift in policy discourses at an international level. The Organisation for Economic Co-operation and Development (OECD) has led the charge in this area with its 'Better Life' initiative. Chapter 4 provides a critique of this new language of wellbeing, arguing that it has, in the hands of bodies such as the Productivity Commission and the OECD, been too tightly wedded to a neoliberal view of the world. 'Wellbeing' has been harnessed to reinforce the push for economic and educational performance, and has now become yet another dimension for competition between nations. Promoting wellbeing in these narrow terms can play a part in keeping citizens 'happy' with the status quo – with modes of life structured by neoliberal global capitalism. I suggest that tertiary education has an important role to play in creating a certain kind of *un*happiness: a sense of discomfort, of uneasiness and restlessness. Attending a tertiary institution such as a university should unsettle comfortable assumptions, challenge prevailing views, and prompt students to ask searching questions of themselves and the world around them. The chapter points to further philosophical scholarship, within and beyond the field of Education, that provides a more rounded, complex and critical perspective on happiness and wellbeing.

With Chapter 5, the philosophical aspects of the book begin to come more to the fore. This chapter argues that in the 21st century philosophy of education has experienced both the best of times and the worst of times. Taking one organisation – the Philosophy of Education Society of Australasia (PESA) – as an example, I show that in a neoliberal world, the field has, in many ways, suffered greatly. In Australia and New Zealand, there are now few university positions advertised specifically in philosophy of education. There is typically very little philosophical content in teacher education programmes, and the presence of philosophy of education courses in the liberal arts has also declined. The questions raised by philosophers of education are seldom appreciated by institutional leaders, and they are almost completely ignored in tertiary education policy documents. Yet, the last two decades have also witnessed a resurgence in scholarship in this domain of study, with journals that are flourishing and strong growth in conference participation. In PESA, younger scholars have been mentored into the Society by older hands and are now, in turn, ushering others into new philosophical conversations. PESA members have been active in bringing philosophical knowledge to bear on the critique of policy. Negotiating the tensions between what is 'best' and what is 'worst' in the current moment speaks to the need to go beyond philosophy of education as understood and practised in university positions. As signalled earlier, I make a case for the view that philosophy of education is a *way of life*, fleshing out what this means through much of the second half of the chapter.

Chapter 6 provides an alternative to the dominant trends examined in the first four chapters of the book. It does so via the work of the Brazilian educationist, Paulo Freire. Freire has been widely acknowledged as a pivotal figure in the field of critical pedagogy. He developed a robust ontological, epistemological and ethical framework to support his pedagogical ideas, drawing on his extensive practical experience as an adult educator in doing so. In his later years, Freire repeatedly expressed concern over the growing encroachment of neoliberal ideas into economic and social life. He was highly critical of the philosophical and political assumptions underpinning policy reforms of the kind explored in this book. Two other influential critical pedagogues, both of whom acknowledged their profound debt to Freire, are Ira Shor and bell hooks. The chapter provides a brief discussion of key insights from Shor and hooks, with a particular focus on the theme of teaching. All three thinkers offer clear points of contrast with the dehumanising and dystopian characteristics of our age; collectively, they help us to see that education can be grounded in a humanising philosophy of hope, combining rigorous critique of the present with the promise of a better tomorrow.

The final chapter pulls various threads from across the book together in a personal account of philosophy of education as a way of life. Exploring autobiographical terrain is, for this author at least, uncomfortable and unusual, but making an exception on this occasion provides one avenue for seeing how policy, philosophy and pedagogy can become intertwined in an academic career. The chapter provides a brief overview of schooling experiences, early encounters with educational philosophy, and subsequent attempts to 'make sense of it all' through writing and teaching. The chapter suggests that philosophy of education makes life more complicated and difficult but also more fulfilling. Living and working as a philosopher of education means being prepared to accept a certain kind of restlessness as fundamental to the process of seeking to understand ourselves, others and the wider world. The sensation of never quite being settled is heightened by the relentless demands of performativity

FROM POLICY TO PHILOSOPHY

and the dehumanising impact of neoliberal policy reforms. But even when the current emphasis on competition and consumption, on managerialism and measurement, has died down, a commitment to this way of life will continue to pose searching questions and problems to be addressed. Philosophy of education helps us to appreciate that we are necessarily unfinished beings. Maturity and experience may allow us to see some things a little more clearly, but there is, at any age, always more educational work to do.

Notes

1 On post-neoliberalism, see Grugel and Riggirozzi (2012); Hall et al. (2013); Lather (2020); Lewkowicz (2015); Springer (2015). For a range of perspectives on performativity, compare Ball (2003); Holloway and Brass (2018); Kenny (2017); Locke (2015); Lyotard (1984); Marshall (1999); McKenzie (2001); Peters (1994); Roberts (2006, 2007a). On education and the changing role of knowledge in contemporary societies, see Blackmore (2001); Bullen et al. (2004); Dawson (2020); Gilbert (2005); Hellström and Raman (2001); Holmwood (2014); Olssen and Peters (2005); Peters and Besley (2006); Roberts (1998a, 2004, 2005); Shore and Taitz (2012); Stiglitz (1999); Ward (2012); Wright and Shore (2018).

2 See, among many other sources, Biebricher (2018); Bottrell and Manathunga (2019); Bourdieu (1998); Davies (2016); Dean (2014); Deem and Brehony (2005); Deem et al. (2007); Flew (2014); Giroux (2002, 2005, 2008); Harvey (2005); Jessop (2002); Klikauer (2015); Kumar (2016); Law (2019); Olssen (2001, 2004); Peck (2010); Peters (2011); Peters and Marshall (1996); Peters and Roberts (1999); Roberts and Peters (2008); Shepherd (2018); Sims (2020); Small (2011); Stolz (2017); Torres (2009); Watts (2016); Whyte and Wiegratz (2016); Wilson (2017); Yeatman and Costea (2018); Zepke (2017).

3 In New Zealand the term 'tertiary education' is employed to cover all post-secondary educational institutions and organisations, including universities, polytechnics, wānanga, industry training organisations, and private training establishments. My main focus in this book, however, is on universities. The terms 'tertiary education' and 'higher education' will thus be used interchangeably.

CHAPTER 1

Performativity, Big Data and Higher Education

The Death of the Professor?

1 Introduction

Jean-Françios Lyotard's *La Condition Postmoderne: Rapport sur le Savoir* first appeared in 1979, a date that now, in our fast-paced world, seems almost a lifetime ago. Published in English translation in 1984, *The Postmodern Condition: A Report on Knowledge* (Lyotard, 1984) has become a classic reference point for those seeking to understand pivotal changes in late 20th century culture and thought. Writing well before the rise of the Internet as a medium of mass communication, Lyotard could see that new language-based technologies would have far-reaching consequences for higher education. In contexts where knowledge was regarded as a commodity, and where the question of truth was becoming subservient to the question of what sells, the importance of university teachers would increasingly be questioned. We would, Lyotard predicted, see the death of the age of the Professor. In the decades that followed the publication of *The Postmodern Condition*, many of the trends observed by Lyotard have become cemented in policy and practice.

This chapter argues that while the age of the Professor is not yet dead, it is *dying*. This has been a slow, steady, often unnoticed process, more evident in some fields than others. Given the dominance of economic goals in shaping educational agendas, the triumph of the performativity principle, and the obsession with measuring and marketing almost everything, support for scholars in the humanities has been progressively eroded. In the era of 'big data', study in the liberal arts, under the guidance of a teacher who seeks knowledge for its own sake rather than its exchange value, can seem like a quaint ideal – a relic of an almost forgotten past. This process of dying is, however, by no means complete, and a rebirth of the age of the Professor, perhaps in a slightly different form, remains a possibility that should not be ruled out.

2 Knowledge, Performativity and the Death of the Professor

Two features of *The Postmodern Condition* have been particularly influential in shaping subsequent scholarship: first, Lyotard's definition of the postmodern

© KONINKLIJKE BRILL NV, LEIDEN, 2019 | DOI:10.1163/9789004518179_002

as 'incredulity toward metanarratives' (Lyotard, 1984, p. XXIV), and second, his discussion of changes in higher education in computerised societies. These two areas of influence – one more self-evidently philosophical, the other more directly relevant to policy – are, of course, closely related. The point of connection between them is Lyotard's account of changes in the nature, status and function of knowledge. *The Postmodern Condition* is not a philosophical treatise on knowledge but neither is it merely a 'report' as suggested by the sub-title of the book. Instead, Lyotard provides a contextualised epistemology, relevant to the problems of his time but with much that still rings true today.

The hypothesis underpinning *The Postmodern Condition* is that in a post-industrial and postmodern age, the status of knowledge changes (p. 3). Lyotard distinguishes between two forms of knowledge, narrative and scientific, arguing that in computerised societies, it is the latter that has come to dominate over the former. This process has been underway from the late 19th century and accelerated with the emergence of new language-based technologies in the second half of the 20th century. Modern sciences and fields of knowledge have relied on appeals to grand narratives 'such as the dialectics of Spirit, the hermeneutics of meaning, the emancipation of the rational or working subject, or the creation of wealth' (p. XXIII). But with metaphysics and the university in crisis, grand narratives have lost the authority they once had and have been replaced by 'narrative language elements' (p. XXIV). We live in and through these heterogeneous language elements, playing different language games. Instead of universals – ethical principles that apply to all, heroes for all cultures and contexts, goals that inspire everyone – there is a focus on the little and the local, the particular and the specific. Postmodern knowledge 'refines our sensitivity to differences and reinforces our ability to tolerate the incommensurable' (p. XXV).

Lyotard identifies a central problem for knowledge: that of legitimation. Legitimation has to do with how authority is exercised to make something – e.g., a law, or a scientific utterance – acceptable. In the process of legitimation, knowledge and power are intertwined. Power is exercised in deciding not only what counts as knowledge but also in determining what needs to be decided (p. 9). In science, Lyotard points out, there has traditionally been a strong connection between research and teaching (pp. 24–25). Scientists pass on their knowledge to others who are expected, in time, to acquire similar expertise to their teachers. Where in the beginning it is assumed that one knows and the other does not, over time the student's view of the teacher changes. Students become aware that their teachers too are still learning; in this manner, they are inducted into the dialectics of scientific research (p. 25). Scientific knowledge, like narrative knowledge, relies on 'moves' in a game structured by a set of generally accepted rules. What counts as a good move in the realm of narrative knowledge cannot be judged by the rules that apply in science, and vice versa. For Lyotard, the diversity of different discourses is something to be valued, with a sense of wonder, just as we might marvel at diversity in the plant or animal kingdom (p. 26). In practice, however, such an attitude tends not to prevail. Those who work in the narrative realm, accepting the limits of their knowledge, may display a certain tolerance towards science, but the reverse does not apply. For the scientist, narrative knowledge is seen as primitive and underdeveloped, as mere opinion or custom; it is based on ignorance and prejudice (p. 27). The inequality between the two forms of knowledge is consistent with the broader history of cultural imperialism in the West. What makes this particular kind of imperialism distinctive is that it is driven by the legitimation imperative. Science, despite its rejection of narrative knowledge, remains dependent on it. The very act of asserting its superiority, its truth, relies upon a narrative of legitimation.

The abandonment of metanarratives in postmodernity poses problems not just for those who work with narrative knowledge but for scientists as well. Boundaries between disciplines are breaking down, new fields are emerging, and in place of the old hierarchy of subjects a new 'flat' structure of different domains of inquiry appears. The crisis faced by scientific knowledge is reflective of a broader challenge to the legitimating power of knowledge. In postmodernity, speculative philosophy and humanistic narratives prove less persuasive than they have been in the past, but so too does science. Knowledge in the post-industrial age has become an 'informational commodity' (p. 5): a key force of production and a pivotal element in the quest for power. Conceived in this way, knowledge is desirable not so much for its truth value as its exchange value; it is something to be sold, traded and purchased, in the same manner as other commodities in a competitive marketplace. The twin processes of commodification and computerisation contribute to an exteriorisation of knowledge from knowers (p. 4). What matters is not knowledge itself, or the presence of a knowing subject, but what knowledge can *do*.

When knowledge is understood in this way, the performativity principle – enhancing efficiency by maximising outputs relative to inputs (cf. Locke, 2015, p. 248) – becomes paramount. A move in the language game of technology is considered desirable not because it is just or beautiful but because it minimises energy expenditure (Lyotard, 1984, p. 44). Technology can play an important role in generating revenue, while fields of inquiry based on narrative knowledge become increasingly marginalised. In a world where 'whoever is wealthiest has the best chance of being right' (p. 45), the arts and humanities are regarded as worthless. In the global battle for economic domination, access to, and control over, information becomes vital. Under such conditions, nation states can come to be seen as a hindrance to the circulation and exchange of knowledge in its commodified form, and multinational corporations become ever more powerful. Existing differences between 'developed' and 'developing' nations will be exacerbated, and with advances in technology, many of the functions currently performed by human beings will be taken over by machines. The goal of higher education becomes one of optimising its contribution to 'the performativity of the social system' (p. 48).

If it is accepted that there is an 'established body of knowledge', questions arise as to what from that body of knowledge is to be transmitted, to whom, in what ways, and with what consequences or effects (p. 48). The answers to these questions are important in shaping how a university works. In each case, under contemporary conditions, the performativity criterion is applied. Particular attention is paid to the development of two kinds of skills: first, those aimed at global competitiveness, and second, those focused on maintaining internal social cohesion (p. 48). In the past, the latter would have been built upon an emancipation narrative, but that will no longer suffice; universities are now tasked with supplying people who will be able to fulfil pragmatic roles in the social system. The ends of higher education become functional rather than idealistic. The model of the 'democratic' university, premised on humanist assumptions about the emancipatory power of education, offers 'little in the way of performance' (p. 49). While universities will continue to prepare people for the professions, they will also increasingly take on the task of retraining those already in the workforce. If enhancing the system's performance is the overriding goal, experimentation within the institution will be seen as of little value and will be left to networks outside the university (p. 50).

While the specific ways in which universities respond to these challenges will vary, the overall effect of the performativity principle is to render higher educational institutions subordinate to 'existing powers' (p. 50). If knowledge is no longer sought for its own sake, there is no need for its transmission to be seen as the exclusive preserve of academics (p. 50). The idea of university autonomy has, Lyotard suggests, already been compromised by the fact that teachers in institutions of higher education do not determine their own budgets; they can only allocate funds assigned to them by others. From a functionalist perspective, universities transmit 'an organized stock of established knowledge' (p. 50), a task that need not be reliant on a Professor standing in front of students. If learning can be translated into a computer language, the didactic function of the university could be given over to machines. The machines would, Lyotard imagines, link 'traditional memory banks' such as libraries and 'computer data banks' to 'intelligent terminals placed at the students' disposal' (p. 50). There would still be a place for teaching of certain kinds in such a system: people would, for example, be needed to show others how to use the intelligent terminals. Training in informatics and telematics could, from this perspective, be seen as a useful addition to the university curriculum. Technical skills of this kind have a more obvious connection with improvements in efficiency and performance than knowledge of what is 'true' or 'untrue', or 'just' or 'unjust', and will thus be highly valued (p. 51).

Objections to the partial replacement of human beings by machines are, Lyotard maintains, a reflection of the grand narratives on which we rely to legitimate our activities (p. 51). If appeals to emancipatory or humanistic narratives are no longer needed to justify decisions made and actions taken, this shift in the means for transmitting knowledge will not present itself as a problem. In contexts where the key drivers are power, performance and control, such narratives prove inadequate and irrelevant in motivating learners to acquire knowledge (p. 51). Lyotard envisages a growing need for people with operational competence, and those who possess such skills will be in high demand (p. 51). Making efficient and strategic use of data to solve immediate problems will be seen as particularly valuable. Knowledge in the postmodern condition can be conceived as a game of 'perfect information', with data, in theory at least, being no longer the exclusive preserve of scientific specialists but available to an expert in any field (p. 52). In such games, the advantage rests with those who can arrange and connect data in new ways. If all players are equally competent, it is 'imagination' – the ability to 'make a new move' or to 'change the rules of the game' – that matters (p. 52). 'Brainstorming' and teamwork can be harnessed to improve performance, while the development of imaginative minds may remain the preserve of a privileged few. In both cases, however, delegitimation and performativity will sound 'the knell of the age of the Professor' (p. 53). The transmission of established knowledge can be left to 'memory bank networks' and 'new moves or new games' can be imagined by interdisciplinary teams (p. 53). Professors, Lyotard implies, will not merely be seen as unnecessary; they may, in the quest for efficiency, be regarded as a hindrance to progress. Their knowledge and experience will be devalued or disregarded, and they will 'die' along with the humanistic narratives that once sustained them.

3 Higher Education in the Age of Big Data

Over the years, *The Postmodern Condition* has attracted a good deal of attention from educationists (see, for example, Gietzen, 2010; Irwin, 2018; Koller, 2003; Lange, 2015; Locke, 2015; Marshall, 1999; Nuyen, 1992; Peters, 1989, 1995,

1997, 2006; Roberts, 1998a; Usher, 2006; Zembylas, 2000), and key questions addressed in the book remain as relevant in our present age as they were in Lyotard's time. Two decades ago, in reflecting on Lyotard's work, it was possible to claim: 'In one sense, the full impact of computerisation has yet to be felt in the tertiary sector: academics have not yet been replaced (at least not in large numbers) by machines. Given what we know to be possible (in terms of processing power and technical sophistication) there is at present only rather limited use of the sort of data exchange systems envisaged by Lyotard' (Roberts, 1998a, p. 5). Is this still true today? Yes and no. We continue to have universities, as physical spaces with campus grounds and buildings. On those campuses there are academic staff (faculty), who teach students on a face-to-face basis in classrooms, laboratories and lecture theatres. Professors are very much alive and well, with a presence not only in students' lives but in the wider world, with their expertise still in demand, in some fields at least, in the media, by governments, and in the corporate world. Professors and other faculty members are more active than ever in research, prompted in part by some of the trends foreshadowed by Lyotard's analysis – in particular, the emergence of new performance-based research funding regimes. Yet, death and dying, in a symbolic sense, are everywhere in the contemporary university. These changes are, in part, a reflection of developments in online education, but they also signal deeper shifts in the way power is exercised across the globe. The process of commodifying knowledge, and of reconfiguring higher education in accordance with the performativity principle, is an incomplete project, as the discussion below attempts to demonstrate.

The development of MOOCs – Massive Open Online Courses – provides an interesting contemporary example of what might be termed a partial victory for performativity. MOOCs are a kind of hybrid, both relying on Professors and dispensing with them. Professors may provide the initial content, through lectures or other forms of teaching that do not look too dissimilar to the pedagogical approaches adopted in an earlier era. But once this material has been recorded, it is then distributed widely – 'beyond' the Professor – via online platforms. As Longstaff (2017, p. 314) observes, '[t]hrough a modular, online, video-based format, MOOCs offer a way for universities to market their wares to a global audience on an unprecedented scale, at little to no cost to participants'. Some commentators distinguish between well-financed, teacher-focused 'xMOOCs', with an emphasis on 'knowledge duplication', and learner-focused 'cMOOCs', where knowledge is created in a more organic way via connections between students (cf. Baggaley, 2013, p. 371; Billsberry, 2013, p. 741; Guardia, Maina and Sangra, 2013, p. 2). MOOCs of both kinds have spread rapidly, generating considerable popular interest in their impact on conceptions and practices of education. This was evident some years ago, for instance, when *The New York Times* declared 2012 to be the year of the MOOC (Evans and McIntrye, 2016, p. 313). MOOCs deal with student numbers that are truly mind-boggling. In 2011, two academics at Stanford University provided open access to their course on Artificial Intelligence, and attracted 58,000 students (Howarth et al., 2016, p. 75). The same university reported enrolments of over 300,000 students across three computer courses (Billsberry, 2013, p. 740). There are now hundreds of institutions in partnership with Coursera, edX and Udacity, delivering MOOCs to more than 10 million participants worldwide (Longstaff, 2017, p. 315).

Enrolment numbers in many MOOCs may be staggeringly high by 'age of the Professor' standards, but completion rates are low, averaging only about 13% (Howarth et al., 2016, p. 75). Moreover, despite hopes that MOOCs might play an important part in the process of lifting people out of poverty – an affordable way of allowing people to secure the knowledge they need to gain employment or improve in their existing jobs (Evans & McIntrye, 2016, p. 314) – in practice it has been the 'wealthiest, most educated citizens of developing nations' who have been most likely to take these courses (p. 315). MOOCs are still evolving, but at present they remain in an ambiguous position when considered against the backdrop of Lyotard's knell of the age of the Professor thesis. Some have been set up with contributions from Professors at prestigious universities such as Harvard, MIT and Stanford, but others have emerged as for-profit start-ups (cf. Jona & Naidu, 2014, p. 141). Some might be seen as a genuine attempt to democratise knowledge; others merely serve as 'shop windows' for universities – designed to enhance their 'brand' in a competitive marketplace. MOOCs could become a key means for enacting the performativity principle and accelerating the relentless drive for efficiency, but if the academic standards they uphold are to be high, they are expensive (and in that sense, 'inefficient') to develop. In addition to Professors or other academic staff, they can require 'a film or TV director, an editor, animators, designers, lighting engineers, web design engineers, actors, and educational designers' (Billsberry, 2013, p. 744).

We need, however, to dig a little deeper than this and ask ourselves exactly what has 'died', or is in the process of dying, in higher education. A clue to answering this question lies in the precise wording of Lyotard's statement on the fate of the Professor. He refers to the *knell* of the *age* of the Professor. 'Knell' in its noun form means the sound made by the slow, solemn ringing of a bell, typically to mark a death – hence the frequent conjoining of the two terms as 'death knell'. Lyotard is thus providing a *signal* of a death – one that he believes will be greeted with a certain solemnity or sadness. But it is not the Professor him- or herself who has died here; it is the *age* to which the Professor belongs. Lyotard's point, then, is not so much that there will be an immediate or literal withering away and eventual complete disappearance of the Professoriate; rather, he is sounding a note to signal the dying of a period in history. The 'age' of the Professor includes the practices, the attitudes, and the forms of life characteristic of that historical moment. This is an age that spans a period of about 1000 years, to the birth of the medieval university, but its roots go much deeper than this – in the West, to the ancient Greeks and the founding of Plato's academy, and in the East perhaps even further than this. The idea of having specialised forms of esteemed knowledge, held by relatively few people and passed on via rigorous training, mentoring and study, stretches back millennia, and given this deep history, is unlikely to simply evaporate. Traces of the idea will remain, no matter how radical and far-reaching policy and political changes may be. So, it is more correct, perhaps, to speak of the 'death' of the Professor not as a single, terminal event, but rather as an ongoing, multifaceted process of *dying*.

The distinctively *modern* expression of the ancient forms of cultural and intellectual life that have created the 'age of the Professor' has, as Lyotard points out, a strong humanist and emancipatory thrust. It is tied to Enlightenment notions of knowledge setting us free. Knowledge liberates us, both in a manner that is visible externally, by opening up opportunities that would otherwise be closed, and in an inner sense, by freeing the mind to realise its fuller potential. Knowledge, on the Enlightenment view, is inextricably linked with the activities of individual conscious human agents. 'Knowing' is a *human* activity, and the transmission of knowledge is something that occurs from one person to another (or many others). Lyotard's prediction that knowledge would increasingly be produced in order to be sold has, over the decades, proven to be uncannily accurate. 'Knowledge' in the traditional, humanistic sense has been both problematised and marginalised. Its commodified form, as information with an exchange value traded between 'sellers' and 'buyers', has become ever more prominent, both within and beyond universities. Yet, the transition that Lyotard describes is by no means complete. Knowledge of the more traditional humanistic kind is, in many contexts, under threat, even under 'siege' (cf. Nussbaum, 2010), and is in that sense 'dying', but it has not completely disappeared. Lyotard recognised that scientific knowledge relies on narrative knowledge for its own justification, but there is more to it than that. In contemporary higher education, the narratives harnessed to justify institutional changes – ironically, sometimes including those most at odds with the traditional ideal of the university – bear the definite imprint of the humanistic knowledge most at risk in the age of performativity.

Most universities publish 'vision statements' and 'strategic plans', and the language employed in such documents frequently draws on emancipatory ideals espoused in earlier times. It is not uncommon, for example, for these statements to refer, in one way or another, to students and/or faculty members 'making a difference' in the world, and this is assumed to be a *worthwhile* difference. In the policy documents developed by government bodies too, there remain traces of the very form of knowledge most evidently lacking in the content and overall direction of the policy. The last version of New Zealand's *Tertiary Education Strategy* before a change of government in 2017 (New Zealand Government, 2014) provides an example. Like many documents of this type, the *Strategy* places a heavy emphasis on the need for tertiary education to contribute to international economic competitiveness. It stresses the principle of 'performance' as the driver for institutional and individual academic activity, and it pushes tertiary education organisations to respond to the demands of employers and markets. The social benefits of tertiary education barely warrant a mention, and it is as if those who write such statements barely know what to say when speaking about such benefits. The humanities are conspicuous by their absence in the *Strategy*, and it is clear that they are accorded little importance. As if to leave no doubt about where it was believed our efforts should be focused, a 'Productivity Commission' was established, and it was left to that body to produce the only substantial government-funded document on tertiary education during National's nine years in power from 2008 to 2017 (New Zealand Productivity Commission, 2017).

The message to those who work in the sector is clear: perform, produce and prosper. This reinforces the dominance of economics in shaping higher education policy, a trend that has been underway for more than two decades (Fitzsimons, Peters & Roberts, 1999). And yet, for all that, humanistic knowledge has not been entirely extinguished. It remains in the voices that sit on the edges of policy – that frame it and preface it and promote it. The statements made in the Forewords produced by Ministers (or their officials) in strategy documents often contain fragments of the older discourse that is most under threat in the era of performativity. They will sometimes speak of values and principles that seem radically at odds with the stark messages conveyed in the substance of a policy document. Press statements also frequently hark back to an earlier era in the language they use to 'sell' a new policy direction. Even references to the most tired and vacuous of policy terms – 'relevance', 'quality' and the like (Ministry of Education, 2006, 2009) – have an epistemological heritage that is seldom acknowledged but still sitting quietly in the background. Humanistic knowledge, in short, may be under attack or devalued or ignored, but it finds its way into even the most unlikely of policy places. It is, we might say, being *put* to death but is refusing to die easily.

In New Zealand, universities have a statutory obligation, under an amendment to the Education Act of 1989, to accept a role as 'critic and conscience of society'. This role receives little or no direct discussion in most government policy documents on tertiary education, yet it provides some protection for academics who wish to voice concerns about the economic and social direction the country is taking (Roberts, 2007b). But even without a legislative warrant of this kind, academics are unlikely to be entirely silent. The overall thrust of the reform process, across the Western world, has been broadly in accordance with Lyotard's predictions, but dissent has not disappeared. Indeed, some of the developments foreshadowed by Lyotard have themselves provided the means for mustering collegial support in resisting the reforms. The computerised terminals in Lyotard's analysis might be seen as a sketch of what was to come with the Internet, and whatever else the Internet does, it at least has the potential to allow Professors, students and social activists to connect, engage and organise with others, all over the world, with a speed and efficiency that could barely have been imagined just a few decades ago. Lyotard saw that computerisation could assist groups in 'discussing metaprescriptives' by providing the information that would usually be lacking in making 'knowledgeable decisions' (Lyotard, 1984, p. 67). He favoured an opening up of the 'data banks', allowing free access to knowledge – with its inexhaustible reserve of possible utterances – for all members of the public. Language games would, he maintained, then become 'games of perfect information at any given moment' (p. 67). Yet he also envisaged the prospect of computerisation becoming something much more sinister in a market system: an instrument of terror that would control and regulate knowledge in accordance with the performativity principle. To date, neither of these scenarios has fully come into being. Elements of both are evident, but the stark 'either/or' set of possibilities signalled by Lyotard has not yet eventuated.

Lyotard's statement on dual possibilities in the computerisation of society appears at the very end of *The Postmodern Condition*. This is arguably both the most important and the weakest part of the book. His brief comments on opening up the data banks are offered as a brief sketch of a politics that 'would respect both the desire for justice and the desire for the unknown' (p. 67), yet the reader is ill-prepared for a normative claim of this kind. Indeed, the appeal to justice seems at odds with the critique of modernist, humanist narratives that appears earlier in the book. By positing incredulity toward metanarratives as the hallmark of a postmodern frame of mind, and by implying that this is the epistemological and ethical orientation he favours, Lyotard places himself in something of a bind. Attempts to cast him as a supporter of the neoliberal trends he identifies (cf. Mack, 2014) are misplaced, but Lyotard leaves himself exposed to such criticism given his refusal to speak definitely of these developments as unjust or undesirable. His ethical and political ideas were developed more fully elsewhere (Lyotard, 1988, 1993), and, taken collectively, those writings provide a clearer picture of what he might have to say in responding to neoliberalism. In *The Postmodern Condition* his ostensible concern is more specific: he is completing a commissioned report. Still, regardless of the status and purpose of *The Postmodern Condition*, Lyotard cannot, given his tacit espousal of a relativist moral position, make a strong case to show that the changes discussed in his narrative are ethically 'wrong' or undesirable. We do not need to be so cautious. Despite the fact that the victory of the performativity principle is not complete, and the age of the Professor is not yet dead, there are deeply worrying signs.

These have to do, in large part, with the growing influence (predicted by Lyotard) of multinational corporations over everyday lives. In particular, it is the enormous power exercised by tech giants such as Google that must be problematised, questioned and contested. Google plays a key role in 'regulating' and 'controlling' the circulation of information along the lines envisaged by Lyotard. Universities, along with other educational institutions, have felt the effects of 'Googlisation' (cf. Peters, 2012; Vaidhyanathan, 2009). Control is established via the vast quantities of data collected through its search engine, and by the way those employing the engine are directed to some sites as their first choices over others. Preferences are shaped by the advertising dollars Google collects from other corporates, such that the 'language games' played by those surfing the Internet are far from neutral. They are not, in Lyotard's terms, games of perfect information. Tastes, preferences, attitudes, decisions, and actions can all be heavily influenced by where browsers' eyes are directed as they undertake searches on the Internet. Of course, other search engines can be employed, but Google's technical sophistication, its aggressive promotion of its own products, and its global dominance make it difficult for competitors to win over potential browsers. It is not just the sheer volume of data that is significant here; it is also what Google does with the data. Default privacy settings provide a remarkably low level of protection for browsers. Searches are stored and, over time, with the application of complex algorithms, patterns of browsing activity create a picture of an individual's wants, interests and possible purchases. Those browsing the Internet may think they are invisible, but many of their physical characteristics (e.g., their approximate age and their gender) will quickly become evident. Information is being traded and exchanged under such a system, but not on an equitable basis.

The changes that were already underway in Lyotard's time in separating 'knowledge' from 'knowers' have continued, on multiple fronts, and this has contributed to a progressive dying away of *being* in favour of *having*. Performance-based systems of research assessment have not only contributed to ongoing productivity among academics in their publishing activities but have also played a role in advancing the commodification of knowledge and replacing it with the idea of performance (Roberts, 2006, 2007a). To perform under such schemes, it is not necessary to demonstrate what one knows, or why, or even that one knows at all. Nor is there any requirement to show that one has taught others how or why to know. The emergence of performance-based research funding is consistent with the wider encroachment of cultures of measurement in university life. Teaching is frequently reduced to the same logic, with 'teaching effectiveness' supposedly being determined by student ratings on 5-point scales. Such tendencies are evident on a much larger scale, with international league tables that rank universities against each other (e.g., the QS and Times Higher rankings) and global testing regimes such as PISA that compare one country against another in school performance across different subject areas (see further, Lynch, 2015; Sellar & Lingard, 2014). League tables of this kind have been heavily criticised, but they seem to be here to stay. They generate considerable anxiety at all levels in the education system and more widely, from individual students and teachers to institutional leaders and politicians. Over the last two to three decades, measurement has increasingly been viewed as very much a *positive* influence in education: a way of generating greater certainty in assessing progress and in determining priorities for the investment of limited resources (cf. Roberts, 1997a; Webster, 2017). In the contemporary world, the obsession with measurement is by no means limited to education. With the widespread use of social media, for instance, value and status are frequently construed in terms of the number of hits a website receives or the number of subscribers a You Tube account has obtained.

The emergence of discourses on 'evidence' in education (e.g., claims that teaching should be 'evidence-based') is a further exemplification of these trends. It converges with the growing application of 'big data' analytics and algorithmic thinking within education and more broadly (see further, Argenton, 2017; Attaran, Stark & Stotler, 2018; Ben-Porath & Shahar, 2017; Cope & Kalantzis, 2015; Daniel, 2015; Eichhorn & Matkin, 2016; Peters, 2012; Petrilli, 2018; Prinsloo, 2017; Schouten, 2017; Thompson, 2017; Wang, 2017; Williamson, 2017, 2018). With the aid of powerful computers and search engines, vast quantities of data can now be sifted, sorted, packaged, and produced. Huge data sets can be employed to inform policy decisions, structure educational interventions, and prioritise the spending of public funds. Lyotard foresaw that access to and control over information would be a critical factor in battles for global power in the future, and in the world of big data this struggle for domination can be played out in a particularly dramatic way. The very label 'big data' itself speaks volumes about what is at stake here; it suggests something large and imposing, a force to be reckoned with. Data can *dominate*, rendering the dissenting individual Professor powerless. The numbers provided through appeals to big data are supposed to speak for themselves. Data may have to be interpreted by human beings, but even that process is increasingly being systematised and streamlined. The aim seems to be to reduce the complexity, the messiness, the unpredictability of education – to remove, as much as possible, the 'human' element from the process. With data at their fingertips, politicians, officials and institutional leaders can feel emboldened – armed, as it were – in making decisions that would otherwise be hard to sell. In the era of big data, questions of ethics are assumed to no longer be relevant or central to the educational process. The dominance of scientific knowledge is being reasserted, bolstered by the 'market knowledge' that sustains neoliberal forms of life (cf. Roberts, 2004).

At one point in *The Postmodern Condition* Lyotard creates the memorable image of the system as 'a vanguard machine dragging humanity after it, dehumanizing it in order to rehumanize it at a different level of normative capacity' (p. 63). Technocrats claim that members of a society cannot know what they need; they are compromised by the fact that they are not 'variables independent of the new technologies' (p. 63). This, Lyotard suggests, betrays both arrogance and blindness. The reference to de/humanisation here is of particular interest given the focus of this book. Lyotard does not elaborate on what humanisation might mean, but the links between his observation and the contemporary world of performance measurement and big data analytics are worthy of further reflection. What we have now, it could be argued, is not so much a 'takeover' by the machines, but something equally problematic from an ethical – and educational – point of view: the creation of increasingly *machine-like* process for the production, conveying and evaluation of academic content. As will be discussed in the next chapter, in performance-based research funding schemes, the language of 'outputs' dominates. Strong incentives are in place to produce more outputs, in better journals, with greater 'impact'. At present, in Britain's Research Excellence Framework and in New Zealand's Performance-Based Research Fund, there is still the important element of peer review, with panels assigned to judge the submitted portfolios of fellow researchers across different disciplinary areas. But this is comparatively expensive and inefficient; it breaks the rules of the performativity principle, and pressure to reduce such costs in time and money and to ease the decision-making process will continue to grow. Removing the human element and replacing this entirely with a numbers-driven system (based, for example, on the number of publications, the ranking of journals, citation counts, the dollars gained in external research income, the number of research students supervised to completion, the hits on a social media account, and so on) would be consistent with changes already underway elsewhere.

The dehumanising character of these changes speaks directly to the theme of death. Dehumanisation can, as Paulo Freire argued (and as will be evident from Chapter 6 in this book), be seen as a life-denying process. It denudes human beings of their dignity and diminishes the place of the unique individual Professor (or student) in academic affairs. In the relentless drive for efficiency, with big data employed to further this end, there is a denial of the distinctiveness of each educational situation. Dehumanisation is destructive: it involves a kind of violence toward, or violation of, something that is worth preserving. The application of the performativity principle is, however, not a sign of strength but of weakness. It represents, among other things, a refusal to pay attention – to the particulars, the interactions, the unexpected developments that give educative moments value and character. Seen in this light, dehumanisation can be a very subtle process. The 'terror' of our current era lies not so much in any sudden, traumatic event but more in the gradual, almost invisible 'wearing down' of academics via managerialist structures and practices. It lies in the small concessions made every day to the logic of performativity. 'Dying' becomes a normal mode of academic being. It is important not to romanticise the past; pressures to 'perform' have always existed. We also need to acknowledge how hard it is to analyse changes while being carried along with them. Nevertheless, in reflecting on the time that has passed since Lyotard wrote *The Postmodern Condition*, it is clear that much of significance has been lost – slowly, steadily, sometimes invisibly. The academy of old cannot ever be fully recovered, but all new eras retain traces of the old and there is no 'pure' transition from one moment in history to the next.

4   Conclusion

If, as has been argued above, what we are witnessing is the *dying* rather than the death of the age of the Professor, the increasing use of numbers, data and systems of performance measurement might be seen as the loudest bell that is currently ringing to signal this dying. The situation remains poised on a knife edge. On the one hand, there is a relentless drive to conform to the dictates of the performativity principle; to reduce knowledge to information, and to remove distracting 'human' elements from the educational process. The power wielded by multinational corporations in managing and manipulating data can, in conjunction with the decisions made by national and international governing bodies, make individual Professors and their students seem irrelevant; they become fodder in the giant machine to which Lyotard refers, being dragged along by it regardless of their individual views of what education can or should be. On the other hand, the new technologies have created fresh opportunities for creative, critical individual and collective work in higher education. A process of dying holds open the possibility of revival or rebirth, if circumstances are favourable for this, and it is possible that a new age of the Professor – in a computerised but not necessarily dehumanised world – will emerge in the years ahead. We cannot know exactly what that age will look like but we can work toward retaining the best from the humanistic university of the past while keeping an open mind about the academy of the future.

Acknowledgement

This chapter was originally published as Roberts, P. (2019). Performativity, big data and higher education: The death of the professor? *Beijing International Review of Education*, *1*(1), 73–91. With permission from Brill (https://brill.com).

CHAPTER 2

Academic Dystopia

Knowledge, Efficiency and Intellectual Life

1 Introduction

The previous chapter drew on Jean-François Lyotard's *The Postmodern Condition* in arguing that the 'age of the Professor' is dying, but not yet dead. Particular attention was paid to the pedagogical implications of Lyotard's analysis. This chapter extends the discussion of Lyotard's work, but with a sharper focus on the theme of research. As noted in Chapter 1, *The Postmodern Condition* has been influential among those with a critical interest in policy, particularly in relation to the university sector. It is not hard to see why the book has had such a lasting impact. It provides a highly prophetic account of sweeping changes in key areas of economic, social and educational life. Lyotard identifies fundamental shifts in conceptions of the nature, function and status of knowledge that would become clearly evident both within and beyond the confines of the academy. His concept of performativity explains a mode of thinking that has become cemented in the bureaucratic mind and embodied in institutional procedures and priorities. His comments on computerisation foreshadow the emergence of the Internet as a phenomenon of profound cultural significance in the last part of the twentieth century. Finally, in his discussion of the shifting role of the state and the rise of multinational corporations, Lyotard depicts a possibility that has become a now taken-for-granted reality in many parts of the world.

Lyotard did not frame his work in terms of the organising themes of utopia or dystopia but *The Postmodern Condition* lends itself readily to analysis from such a perspective. With so much having been written about Lyotard, and *The Postmodern Condition* in particular, it can be helpful to focus on a quite specific context as a means for making some broader theoretical observations. This will be my task in the present chapter. I examine developments in tertiary education and research policy in New Zealand, taking the Performance-Based Research Fund (PBRF) as an example of performativity, competition and the commodification of knowledge in action. I argue that the trends evident in changes under the PBRF constitute a form of academic dystopia. The chapter begins with a brief overview of Lyotard's position on knowledge, efficiency and performativity. This is intended to complement, but not duplicate, the summary

© TAYLOR & FRANCIS, 2013 | DOI:10.1163/9789004518179_003

24   CHAPTER 2

provided in Chapter 1. I then outline the development of performance-based research funding in New Zealand, setting this discussion in the context of the history of neoliberal reform in this country. Finally, I assess the PBRF in the light of Lyotard's ideas. I comment on the limiting language of 'outputs', discuss links between information, interpretation and the 'unknown', and consider the impact of research assessment regimes on intellectual life.

2   Knowledge, Efficiency and Performativity

As we saw in Chapter 1, in *The Postmodern Condition* Lyotard argues that knowledge, rather than being seen as an end in itself, has become a commodity: something to be produced and consumed, creating an exchange value (Lyotard, 1984). Knowledge has become a key force of production, altering relations within and between nations. Science has already asserted its superiority over narrative knowledge, and Lyotard predicts that it will play an increasingly important role in enhancing productivity within individual nations. This will, in combination with other factors, lead to a growing gap between developed and developing countries. In the global struggle for power, knowledge as an informational commodity will be crucial. Under these conditions, the role of the state changes. Multinational corporations will exert an increasing degree of influence over investment decisions, and the state will no longer be seen as necessary in the learning process. With the commercialisation of knowledge, social progress is measured, in part, by the ease with which information – as one form of capital – circulates. Lyotard envisages nation states reconsidering their relations with corporations and civil society. He foresees the opening of world markets and a return to vigorous economic competition.

Lyotard points out that in postmodern technoscientific societies there is a heavy emphasis on *efficiency*. Efficiency is determined by the extent to which an output (the information or modifications obtained) can be maximised with minimum input (the energy expended in the process). The origins of this view of technical competence lie in the first industrial revolution, where the relationship between wealth and technology was established. Investing in technology allows tasks to be completed more efficiently, thereby increasing surplus-value (p. 45). Creating research funds, into which a portion of the sale is recycled, provides one way of further enhancing performance. In this manner, science becomes a 'force of production', a 'moment in the circulation of capital' (p. 45). Support by nation-states and, increasingly, corporations, for applied technological research has been driven by the imperatives of profit and power. A temporary loss (in profit terms) will be tolerated if it is believed that a decisive innovation – and hence a competitive advantage – will result from investment in scientific and technological research. Institutions, organisations and research centres unable to justify their existence on the basis of even an indirect contribution to the optimisation of this system's performance will find diminishing support from the state and the corporate sector. In these circumstances, idealist and humanist narratives no longer serve a legitimating function and will be abandoned as the quest for (global, corporate) power continues.

When the desired goal becomes 'the optimal contribution of higher education to the best performativity of the social system' (p. 48), skills of two kinds become important: those specifically designed to tackle world competition, and those capable of fulfilling a society's own needs, particularly in terms of maintaining internal cohesion. In the past, this task involved 'the formation and dissemination of a general model of life, most often legitimated by the emancipation narrative' (p. 48). In an environment of delegitimation, however, universities and other institutions of higher learning are called upon to create skills rather than ideals. In the future, it will not be a matter of conveying a body of knowledge to all young people as a way of preparing them for work; rather, knowledge will be 'served "a la carte"' to those who are already in the workforce but who wish to upgrade their skills, improve their prospects for promotion, or open up new employment opportunities (p. 49).

These changes signal a decisive shift in the nature of instruction. When knowledge ceases being an end in itself, and becomes merely another commodity in the system, its transmission and circulation need not be largely confined to institutions such as universities. If knowledge is to be acquired not for the advancement of a grand narrative of legitimation but in order to exercise power, new questions arise. Instead of asking 'Is it true?', the focus will shift to other questions such as: 'What use is it?', 'Is it efficient?' and 'Is it saleable?' (p. 51). In contexts shaped by questions of this kind, the hardships citizens suffer are addressed only insofar as their alleviation improves the system's performance. When societies are governed by the imperatives of power and performativity, the needs of the most underprivileged are not met on principle, but only to the extent that not satisfying (some of) them could lead to a destabilising of the system as a whole. Those who exercise power refuse to be ruled by weakness; instead, they redefine the norms of life. Technocrats will arrogantly and blindly decide that they know what is best for society, placing their faith in new technologies in doing so (p. 63).

Such a regime is one of terror. A system of this kind involves the elimination or threatened elimination of other players from a language game. Opponents are silenced or consent, not because they have been refuted, but because their ability to participate has been threatened. Decision-making driven by this form of terror says, in effect, 'Adapt your aspirations to our ends – or else' (p. 64). Lyotard concludes *The Postmodern Condition* with a summary of two possible futures. The computerisation of society could, on the one hand, be driven exclusively by the principle of performativity and become the means through which ever greater control is exercised over the market system. On the other hand, it could also play a part in aiding discussion of metaprescriptives by opening up access to information that would otherwise not normally be available (p. 67). Lyotard appears to favour the second path, on both ethical and epistemological grounds, but, as signalled in the previous chapter, this part of the book is rather light on philosophical and practical detail and it is left to readers to take the conversation further.

3   Performance-Based Research Funding in New Zealand

In the 1980s New Zealand attracted international attention for its wide-ranging program of neoliberal reform. A small democracy with few buffers between government and those directly affected by neoliberal policies, New Zealand was able to implement economic change at a remarkable rate (Peters & Marshall, 1996). The rapidity of the reform process was anything but accidental. Roger Douglas, Minister of Finance in the Labour government of 1984–1987, enshrined the principles of acting quickly and decisively – of making changes in quantum leaps, with minimal time for interest groups to mobilise – in political folklore. Douglas lost the Finance portfolio in Labour's second term in the 1980s as Prime Minister David Lange sought to slow the pace of change – it was time, he felt, for 'a cup of tea' – but with the National Party's landslide election win in 1990 a new phase of the neoliberal restructuring process began.

Where Labour had concentrated on the 'core' economic sector, National seized an opportunity to begin reforming the key social policy domains. During three successive terms in government in the 1990s, National applied a philosophy of marketisation to social welfare, health and education. The principles underpinning marketisation were particularly evident in tertiary education. Tertiary education institutions and organisations were expected to operate like businesses – to apply corporate management practices to their day-to-day activities, to compete with each other, to embrace the language of 'performance indicators' and 'strategic planning', and to advertise aggressively for 'clients' or 'consumers'. National provided strong incentives for the privatisation of tertiary education and created the conditions for a proliferation of new 'providers' of degrees, diplomas, certificates and other qualifications (Olssen, 2001; Peters & Roberts, 1999).

The formation of the Labour-Alliance government in 1999 was greeted by many in the field of education with a sense of relief. Keen to distance itself from both the Rogernomics era of the 1980s and the 'more market' years under National in the 1990s, the new government adopted a 'Third Way' approach to economic and social policy reform, drawing on Tony Blair's experience with New Labour in Britain but with adaptations for the New Zealand context (Codd, 2001; Giddens, 2000; Olssen & Peters, 2005; Roberts & Peters, 2008). Tertiary education was to become a flagship policy area for Third Way thinking. Choice and competition were to be de-emphasised, new forms of collaboration were to be encouraged, and concentrations of research excellence were to be fostered. A more strategic and integrated approach to tertiary education reform would be taken, underpinned by a 'shared vision' of New Zealand's future. Tertiary education, the government promised, would become a key means for advancing New Zealand as a 'knowledge society and economy' (Ministry of Education, 2002).

National was returned to power in late 2008 but, as noted in the previous chapter, did little to deepen and extend policy work on tertiary education. There was a more overt emphasis on productivity, performance and economic advancement, and the language of social inclusiveness largely disappeared, but nothing of substance emerged directly from the government in charting a new, well-informed approach to tertiary education (see Ministry of Education, 2009; New Zealand Government, 2014). With a change back to Labour in 2017, there was a sense that something truly transformative was needed in rethinking the direction of tertiary education policy in New Zealand. To date, this has not eventuated. The government has had to deal with multiple crises, including the global Covid-19 pandemic, and tertiary education has had to take something of a back seat in the face of other more pressing policy concerns (e.g., in health, housing and welfare). A new tertiary education strategy document has been produced, in conjunction with a set of national education and learning priorities, but this is very thin on detail (see Ministry of Education, 2020). Other possible changes in the education system at the school level (e.g., in assessment and curriculum) appear to be more far-reaching in their implications, but it is too early to tell what any new policies will look like in practice.

The PBRF emerged from work undertaken shortly after the Labour-Alliance government of 1999 took office. Determined to forge a new narrative for reform following National's aggressive programme of marketisation in the 1990s, the coalition government announced the formation of a Tertiary Education Advisory Commission (TEAC). Those appointed to serve on this body were tasked with providing a comprehensive review of the tertiary education sector in New Zealand. The Commission produced four reports, varying in length, style and focus (TEAC, 2000, 2001a, 2001b, 2001c). The last and longest of the reports, *Shaping the Funding Framework* (TEAC, 2001c), concentrated on questions of funding and, among other areas, addressed the issue of research. After careful analysis of strengths and weaknesses in the current funding system, together with consideration of research funding regimes elsewhere in the world – particularly Britain's Research Assessment Exercise (RAE) – the report recommended that performance-based research funding be established. The recommendations in the TEAC report were taken further by a Performance-Based Research Fund Working Group (2002). The first assessment round under the new Performance-Based Research Fund was conducted in 2003. A second, partial round was completed in 2006, and full evaluations were conducted in 2012 and 2018.

New Zealand's PBRF includes a number of elements of similar overseas research funding schemes. Individuals in participating tertiary education institutions complete Evidence Portfolios (EPs) with a list of research 'outputs' (e.g., publications and presentations), four of which are nominated as their best. As originally conceived, the outputs section would be the most significant in determining the overall grade (70%), with smaller weightings (15% each) given to two other sections: peer esteem and contributions to the research environment. With each assessment round, EPs have been assessed by expert panels selected by nomination from universities and other tertiary education institutions. In the first quality evaluation, individuals received a grade of 'A', 'B', 'C' or 'R', the first denoting world class research, the last indicating little or no research activity. A new category was introduced in the 2006 round to deal with 'new and emerging' researchers. The key features of the scheme remained largely unchanged in the 2012 and 2018 rounds, though some relatively minor adjustments were made. In 2018, for example, the maximum number of outputs beyond the nominated four best was reduced to 12, and the peer esteem and research contributions components were collapsed into one section. A review has recently been undertaken (PBRF Review Panel, 2020), and although the PBRF is likely to continue, there may be some reasonably substantial changes to the structure and content of evidence portfolios in the future. It seems likely, for example, that more emphasis will be placed on the idea of demonstrating 'impact' in one's research activities. This possible shift follows a move already made in that direction in Britain, as will be discussed in the next chapter.

In the results to date, New Zealand's 'traditional' universities have fared best, ahead of polytechnics, Auckland University of Technology (a 'new' university, formerly Auckland Institute of Technology), and other tertiary education organisations (Tertiary Education Commission, 2004, 2008, 2013, 2019).

ACADEMIC DYSTOPIA 29

Four universities – the University of Auckland, the University of Otago, the University of Canterbury, and Victoria University of Wellington – have featured regularly in the top five on average quality scores. Funding through the PBRF has been based not just on the results of the assessment exercise but also on research degree completions (Masters and doctoral theses) and on externally generated research income. (The review report on the PBRF released in 2020 has proposed that the latter element be eliminated in future rounds.) The older, well-established universities have been dominant in these areas as well. Universities have been quick to exploit their PBRF results, highlighting on their institutional websites and in student and staff recruiting campaigns either their overall supremacy or their performance in particular subject domains. Competition between the top performers has been fierce, with, for example, the University of Auckland the University of Otago engaging in a 'war of words' over the results of the 2006 assessment round. Institutions have devoted a great deal of time and money to the preparation of researchers for the PBRF evaluation exercises, hiring staff specifically to advise and assist in this area. Increasing attention has been paid over more recent years to international measures of research performance, with the league tables produced by the QS and Times Higher assessments exerting the most influence, but the PBRF remains the primary means for securing research funding from government and thus remains firmly the minds of tertiary education leaders.

4   Lyotard, Tertiary Education and the PBRF

Reflecting on Lyotard's account more than four decades on, it seems, in many respects, to have been tailor made as an explanatory framework for New Zealand's approach to economic and social reform. The theme of vigorous international competition remains very much to the fore in New Zealand. Senior Ministers, under both Labour and National governments, have stressed the need for New Zealand to move up OECD tables of economic performance. Knowledge, as Lyotard predicted, has been seen as central to this process (Gilbert, 2005; Roberts & Peters, 2008). Moves have been made to maintain social cohesion after the divisive effects of the market driven policies in the 1990s. At the same time, there has been a push to improve 'efficiency' in New Zealand's government departments and public institutions, with mixed success. At different times, considerable faith has been placed in technology as a means for New Zealand to distinguish itself in commerce and the arts. And, as we have seen, a new research fund – the PBRF – has been created as part of the process of enhancing New Zealand's performance on the international stage.

In its broad outline, then, the picture Lyotard painted four decades ago seems to provide an uncannily accurate portrait of what was to come in this country, and remains as relevant and helpful today as it was then. This does not mean Lyotard's analysis is without its weaknesses, or that *everything* in Lyotard's account holds true. It is acknowledged that other theorists could also have been helpful in evaluating New Zealand's approach to performance-based research funding. Elsewhere, ideas from Foucault (Middleton, 2005) and Nietzsche (Roberts, 2012a), for example, have been employed to frame critical discussions of the PBRF. Other thinkers such as Kierkegaard (Senyshyn, 2005), Marx (Harvie, 2000) and Derrida (Stronach, 2007) have served as reference points in analyses of the RAE in the UK. Lyotard is, however, particularly valuable in getting to grips with changes in the nature and status of knowledge under new conditions of work. What Lyotard offers, and this is not so for (say) Foucault or Nietzsche or Kierkegaard, is a direct focus on the commodification of knowledge, the logic of performativity, and the impact of new information technologies on teaching and research. Lyotard also sets his philosophical analysis in a broader policy context, in a manner that distinguishes him from these thinkers. Most importantly, for present purposes, his portrait of education and society in the postmodern condition speaks powerfully to what can now be seen as an emerging academic dystopia. There is merit, therefore, in pursuing his ideas, while recognising that this provides just one avenue for potentially productive critical inquiry.

4.1 Outputs, Quality and Knowledge

At the heart of the PBRF assessment process is the notion of 'outputs'. While this term is mainly applied in relation to the first section of PBRF evidence portfolios, it has also become common jargon in describing other forms of research work. Thus conceived, an output can be almost any measurable research-related item or activity created or undertaken by an individual or group of individuals. Supporters of the PBRF have been careful not to tie outputs exclusively to the most common forms of academic written work: journal articles, books, chapters in edited collections, technical reports, and the like. In the PBRF, an output can, in theory, also be a musical performance, a play, a painting, a carving, a sculpture, a speech, or a website, among other things, provided there is a demonstrable research component in each case. On the face of it, this appears to be an expansive and inclusive approach to a research evaluation process: one that recognises the many different forms of intellectual work undertaken by those in tertiary education institutions and organisations. Yet, the very idea of conceptualising research activity in terms of outputs is itself limiting. It encourages an instrumentalist approach to research and represents a further step in the process of commodifying knowledge. Of course, the practice of promoting the production of 'outputs' by academics is not new; the 'publish or perish' phenomenon has been a feature of university life in many Western countries for several decades. What distinguishes the current era from earlier times is adoption of a more systematised, standardised means for embodying the principle of 'publish or perish' in a research funding regime and in institutional practice.

Lyotard saw that knowledge in its commodified form becomes virtually indistinguishable from information. Where knowledge in the past might have implied the existence of a knower and something to be known, now neither of these are necessary. Once it has been reconceived as information, knowledge can circulate, be traded and exchanged, without the presence of a knower in any traditional philosophical sense. Knowing, in most schools of epistemological thought, implies something more than mere apprehension or skill in dealing with information. Information takes the form of a product, while knowing is a process. This difference is reflected in the PBRF. Overall, the PBRF demands that research be conceived more in 'product' than 'process' terms. The scheme takes account of the processes involved in undertaking research only insofar as they can be *reconfigured* as products. Thus, publishing a book, supervising a doctoral student, organising a series of research seminars, being invited to give a keynote address, and receiving an award or a favourable review all become products: measurable units to be listed, one by one, as individual outputs or items in an evidence portfolio.

Even where the form of measurement is less explicitly quantifiable than a count of publications or an adding up of dollars earned, the logic is similar. The developers and supporters of the PBRF have, in one sense, accepted that more is not always better. They have stressed the importance of quality over quantity. Yet, with the widespread use of journal rankings and citation indices, qualitative judgments can quickly become quantitative measurements. 'Quality', as has been argued elsewhere (Roberts & Peters, 2008), is one of the most vacuous, ill-defined policy terms. Along with the term 'relevance', it has a long history of unreflective overuse in policy documents. 'Quality policies', as applied in institutions such as universities, are highly problematic (Vidovich & Porter, 1999). Appeals to 'quality' immediately beg further questions: Quality as defined by whom? For what? In relation to what else? Everyone, it seems, supports 'quality', but what is its opposite? In other words, if quality is what is wanted, what is *not* wanted? And, where do the divisions between 'higher' and 'lower' quality lie? The PBRF Evidence Portfolio form simply asks individuals to tick a box indicating whether an 'output' is 'quality assured' or not. Criteria are supplied for determining what counts as 'quality assured', but this somewhat crude, binary division between 'quality assured' and 'non quality assured' does little to inspire confidence that the complexities associated with good judgments about quality have been considered.

The ambiguity associated with the term 'quality' assists in the rhetorical wars over the PBRF. When prospective students see advertisements by universities claiming, on the basis of PBRF results, to employ the highest quality researchers, it is *assumed* that the readers of the advertisements, those being regarded as high quality researchers, and those who assessed the researchers all share the same view of quality. But even if they do not, the effect of the advertisements need not alter. Terms such as 'quality' can still perform the same work in winning over potential students, or corporate backers, or additional government funding, provided no one pauses to problematise the term. In the PBRF, the focus shifts from undertaking research as an end in itself to producing outputs for someone or something else. This move toward a more instrumentalist approach has been under way for some time, as Lyotard noted, but the PBRF pushes it to a new level. Lyotard's principal concern was with changes in the function and status of knowledge; policy developments such as the PBRF prompt a rethinking of the very idea of what it means to be an academic. Lyotard's announcement of the death of the Professor may be proven correct in the longer term, but at present it seems unlikely that either teachers or researchers will be entirely replaced by machines. Nonetheless, there is every possibility, if trends already underway continue, that researchers will be encouraged to become more *machine-like* in their activities. This is a frightening prospect, but it is not inconsistent with other 'terrors' of performativity and neoliberalism (Ball, 2003; Giroux, 2005).

The logic of performativity, Lyotard pointed out, demands that outputs be maximised relative to inputs. Performance-based funding for research provides strong incentives to produce more and more, either in terms in quantity or in terms of quality. Provided overall performance, assessed in these restrictive terms, keeps increasing, intellectual growth becomes irrelevant. Even where individual academics see themselves as researchers driven by strong intrinsic motivations to pursue the truth, or to make new discoveries, or to continue an intellectual conversation, or to pass on what they know to others, the system demands something else from them. The PBRF assessment process does not ask academics to demonstrate, directly and explicitly, depth or breadth in understanding, or to show how their work contributes to an ongoing scholarly dialogue, or to provide evidence that they are committed to the process of knowing. The PBRF does not seek to enter the interior landscape of the academic mind or to ask researchers why they undertake their work. It does not involve talking to those who have been taught or mentored by a researcher.

ACADEMIC DYSTOPIA

Indeed, there is little scope for discussion of any kind by those completing EPS in the PBRF assessment exercise. Narrative knowledge, as Lyotard observed, has become devalued. What the PBRF demands is not a rich, well-rounded, complex portrait of a research life, but simply a *list*. It is measured *performance* that matters, not the knowledge or ideas, research cultures or commitments, that give meaning and substance to lists of items and outputs.

4.2   *Information, Interpretation and the Unknown*

Lyotard's final assessment of possibilities for computerisation is, as suggested in Chapter 1, arguably one of the weakest parts of *The Postmodern Condition*. Reluctant to commit himself fully and overtly to an ethical position, perhaps in part because this would be inconsistent with his critique of metanarratives near the beginning of the book, his preference for 'a politics that would respect both the desire for justice and the desire for the unknown' (Lyotard, 1984, p. 67) remains vague and underdeveloped. He does not provide a robust account of either 'justice' or 'the unknown'. Nor does he explore the ramifications of his political preference for education or research. It is important to contextualise Lyotard's work here. *The Postmodern Condition* was a commissioned report and it was not until later publications such as *The Differend* (Lyotard, 1988) that Lyotard adopted a more deliberate, self-consciously 'philosophical' approach to his work. *The Postmodern Condition* was not a specialist treatise on either politics or ethics. Lyotard's political writings were to appear in another collection, not published in English until 1993 (Lyotard, 1993). All the same, his brief remarks on providing free access to 'the memory and data banks' (Lyotard, 1984, p. 67) are fascinating in the light of subsequent developments in networked computing, and have important implications for educationists in a PBRF environment.

Lyotard was writing more than a decade before the phenomenal growth of the Internet in the 1990s. The Internet certainly has aided some groups in their discussion of 'metaprescriptives' and in some cases has provided such groups with access to information they usually lack for knowledgeable decisions (as Lyotard hoped would be the case with computerisation). But there is no neutral provision of information, and the Internet has furnished plenty of examples of information being used in misleading, defamatory, shallow, or incomplete ways. This is where the importance of education becomes most evident. Lyotard theorised the imminent death of the age of the Professor, yet the need for Professors and other teachers is perhaps more obvious than ever in the age of the Internet. For the challenge now is not so much gaining access to the information, but finding ways of distinguishing some forms of information from others. Teachers, especially at the tertiary level, have a potentially significant role to play in guiding others in this process. As Zygmunt Bauman (1988, 1993) has argued, academics and other intellectuals may have had their status undermined in a marketised world, but they still have something to offer in teaching the 'rules of interpretation'. There is, of course, no *one* approach to interpretation; indeed, this is one of the principal lessons a student or a group can learn from a good teacher. Among the qualities that can be fostered, however, are those with clear value in navigating our way through a sea of information. The development of a searching, probing, investigative, questioning, *critical* frame of mind is arguably vital if the kind of knowledgeable decisions Lyotard had in mind are to be made.

These points have relevance for the PBRF. The volume of official documentation, institutional communication, and academic interaction devoted to the PBRF process has created a sense that these changes to research policy are important, with far-reaching consequences for institutions and individuals. With so much information, retaining a clear picture of the key changes and mechanisms, and a strong sense of control over the process, becomes more difficult. The PBRF process has also added significantly to workloads, with considerable time that might be spent *undertaking* research having been spent on reading and responding to research policy. It is to the Tertiary Education Commission's credit that key documents have been made available to the public, in the manner Lyotard envisaged, via the Internet. But in the face of such a sea of information, it is easy to lose sight of 'bigger picture' questions relating to the PBRF. We can tend to become caught up in the detail, debating differences between subject areas, or the structure of the Evidence Portfolio form, or the composition of the PBRF panels. Discussion at this level may result in minor changes to the way the system operates but it does not contest the underlying ethical and epistemological assumptions behind the PBRF or place it in its broader political context.

Lyotard's references to accessing information and respecting the desire for the 'unknown' hint at something else of importance for researchers. The PBRF does not make knowing – and particularly *knowing for its own sake* – a priority, but neither does it place any substantial value on 'unknowing'. The PBRF can, in some senses, be seen as an attempt to move closer to the ideal of establishing a language game of perfect information. Decisions about grades, to be sure, remain matters of judgment, but the increasing systematisation of the evaluation and preparation processes signals a move to reduce some of the more idiosyncratic and subjective elements of research evaluation. The tendency is toward greater (apparent) certainty for both researchers and evaluators. Work that is 'risky' – that falls outside the usual boundaries for judgment, that takes too long to complete, that questions the very foundations on which the PBRF rests – becomes marginalised. The 'machine-like' nature of PBRF activity, to which I referred earlier, becomes evident here. There are strong incentives in the system for both individuals and the institutions within which they are housed to produce more and more, in ever more predictable ways, with a certain kind of relentless monotony. A perfect PBRF, it might be imagined, would be one where everything could be known: the rules for judgment, the categories for classifying research work, the differences (in precise numerical detail) between institutions in their results, and the extrinsic benefits that might be expected to flow from those results. This would be, perhaps, a perfectly 'just' system in PBRF terms. What is *not* wanted is the messiness, the unpredictability of a system that places a premium on the unknown. This, in the discursive universe of the PBRF, is not merely inefficient but unjust. The implied expectation of the PBRF, and of the broader rhetoric of advancing New Zealand as a knowledge society and economy, is that performance will be improved constantly. For this to occur, planning is necessary, and taking the unknown seriously makes that much more difficult. Lyotard, then, may not have fleshed out his political ideal, but it seems clear that the PBRF is at odds with what he had in mind.

4.3   *Changing Intellectual Lives*

We might agree with TEAC, the PBRF Working Group and successive New Zealand governments that the previous system of funding research – a system based largely on student enrolments – was seriously flawed. This approach to funding encouraged a 'more is better' attitude toward tertiary education and failed to distinguish between institutions that were active in research and those that were not. We might concede that the PBRF is, in *some* respects, a fairer and better means for distributing the limited funds made available for research. We might, moreover, be grateful that New Zealand has not yet gone down the path of measuring research performance purely or largely on the basis of metrics. Reducing the value of a researcher's contribution to citation counts or dollars generated through external funding is, as the next chapter will argue, deeply problematic. Such approaches ignore important differences between fields of study (e.g., in levels of funding available) and paint a radically incomplete picture of research achievements. If the value of performance based research funding is accepted, the PBRF can be seen as better than some of the alternatives.

Yet, none of this ought to deter us from asking fundamental questions about the PBRF specifically and research funding in general in New Zealand: Why is so little money, in international terms, devoted to research in this country? Why is there such a heavy emphasis on improving research 'performance'? What implied theory of knowledge underpins the PBRF? Do the costs, including the human costs, of the PBRF outweigh the potential benefits it might bring? And, crucially, how are we changing as researchers, academics and human beings as a result of our participation in the PBRF process? The last of these questions has been addressed by Ashcroft (2005) and Middleton (2005), among others.

Ashcroft (2005) argues that the PBRF creates a culture of 'winners and losers', with potentially negative consequences for both research and teaching. Researchers, Ashcroft suggests, could become increasingly specialised and less flexible in their research, and less attention could be paid to excellence in teaching. Most worryingly of all, from Ashcroft's perspective, the PBRF could become a key means for distinguishing between academics applying for jobs and seeking promotion. This, Ashcroft believes, will have dire implications, with 'academic collegiality and quality research' giving way to 'widespread career anxiety and apprehension, and more narrowly focused (or constrained) research activity' (p. 125).

Middleton (2005) has conducted empirical research on the impact of the PBRF on academics in the field of Education. Drawing on interviews with 36 researchers evaluated by the Education panel in the 2003 PBRF round, she maintains that academics are being 'disciplined' as subjects in new ways under performance-based research funding. Some received a boost in confidence after receiving good grades, while others experienced considerable anxiety in waiting for the results. Many who were graded at a lower level than expected felt downgraded and discouraged. Those who received 'R' ratings often felt a diminished sense of self-worth. Some, especially older teacher-educators, noted that they were not undertaking research for PBRF grades but because they felt it was important and were less affected by the ratings they received.

Middleton found that the PBRF was already influencing the future goals, strategies and priorities for many Education researchers. Some were becoming 'more calculated, self-conscious, or less spontaneous in their decisions to take on tasks like supervision, reviewing, consultancy or public presentations' (p. 147). Others feared that the PBRF 'could lead to a devaluation of the local in favour of the international, and the academic over the professional' (p. 149). Some senior academics also believed the PBRF was having a negative impact on management and leadership in Education faculties and departments, with fewer people being willing to put their hands up for administrative responsibilities. Middleton concludes that there is already evidence of the PBRF reshaping Education as a field. By insisting on all staff having a researcher identity, 'the PBRF could encourage a downgrading of the grassroots engagements traditionally carried out by Education staff with teachers and classrooms and prioritise for all staff publication in remote, overseas, intellectual journals' (p. 153).

ACADEMIC DYSTOPIA

In a university research environment structured by PBRF requirements, a certain dissonance can become part of our institutional lives. On the one hand, we may develop significant misgivings about the PBRF and its consequences for research and researchers. On the other hand, if we are in senior positions, we may also feel a strong obligation to assist our colleagues, as best we can, to succeed in PBRF terms. After all, jobs, promotions and working conditions are on the line as a result of the PBRF process. There is no easy 'resolution' here, as is true of intellectual life more generally in knowledge economies (Blackmore, 2001; Ozga, 1998). It is possible, however, to see this dissonance as potentially productive. Highlighting the tension, rather than denying it or hiding it, allows some of the contradictions in the PBRF to become more apparent. These are *lived* contradictions, not simply theoretical games, and they are for that reason all the more vivid and instructive. At the same time, if Lyotard is correct in his description of the wider process of change at work here, we must recognise that our very ability to ask critical questions of the PBRF is shaped and limited by the PBRF process itself. Competition, commodification and instrumentalism leave their mark on all of us, even as we interrogate their role in tertiary education and research policy.

5   Conclusion: A Dystopian Future for the Academy?

Lyotard's work offers an important set of signposts for understanding a series of related changes. Collectively, these changes point to a dystopian future for the academy. Lyotard discusses changes in the nature and status of knowledge, the organisational logic under which institutions operate, and commercial relations within and between nations, all of which have come to pass. The forms of surveillance and control Lyotard signalled as possibilities in a computerised world are now no longer the subject of science fiction; as each year goes by, systems for monitoring citizens become more sophisticated, intrusive and widespread. This trend has become more entrenched than ever under the tracing and tracking requirements put in place by governments responding to the Covid-19 crisis. Perhaps the deepest and most far reaching changes, however, are those we often cannot see: subtle but significant shifts in the way we think about ourselves as human beings.

New Zealand's PBRF is part of a wider process of policy reform, where principles at the heart of university life are being undermined. The neoliberal reconstruction of New Zealand has continued, with some variations in emphasis and political style, for the best part of four decades. Neoliberal ideas have held similar sway in many other parts of the world. The ontological heart of neoliberalism is the idea of a self-interested, utility maximising individual who is expected to make continuous consumer-style choices in a competitive world (Codd, 1993; Peters and Marshall, 1996; Roberts, 2014). Over the last three decades, academics have increasingly been encouraged, directly or indirectly, to see themselves in this light, and the PBRF has reinforced this trend. Under the PBRF scheme, competition between institutions is intense, but when finances are tight individuals also become pitted against their colleagues in the race to hold on to their jobs. Redundancies in the Arts and Education have, at different times during the first two decades of the 21st century, been widespread in New Zealand universities. Under such circumstances, research becomes not an integral part of one's being as an academic – the manifestation of a desire to know – but a matter of survival. This can prompt a certain creativity but it can also lead to conformity. Academics can, in Nietzsche's terms, develop a herd-like mentality, and ultimately lose all independence of intellectual spirit (cf. Nietzsche, 1968, 1990, 1997; Roberts, 2012a). In constantly producing for others, we simultaneously reconstitute ourselves. *We* become the 'output': just another cog in the vast machine that is designed to make one country more efficient, more economically competitive than another.

One indication of this can be seen in the new ways we conceive of collective research activity. The notion of a community of scholars has been replaced by the idea of 'research teams', and these are often indistinguishable in many respects from groupings that might be found in the business world. Large university based research teams have highly organised systems for gaining and retaining funding, complex reporting and appointment procedures, and hierarchical management structures. They market themselves, aggressively at times, in a myriad of different ways. These might include, for some or all team members: appearing at the right conferences, contacting the media, meeting officials and Ministers and others with deep pockets, publishing strategically, and repackaging findings to make them more easily understood and palatable. If individual researchers might be said to be becoming more machine-like under the PBRF, research teams can be seen as the embodiment of a factory of well-oiled machines, all working harmoniously in a process of relentless production.

The dystopian character of this unfolding reality is revealed not just in the tendency toward conformity that is built into the PBRF regime but in the propensity among academics to *not* see themselves in this way. Defenders of the PBRF and of the neoliberal turn in tertiary education policy might point to jostling over the meaning of results from earlier assessment rounds, or to questions that are asked about the weightings given to different parts of a portfolio, or to concerns expressed that the scheme favours some tertiary institutions

ACADEMIC DYSTOPIA

over others, as evidence against this claim. How, it might be asked, can the system be seen as conformist when there is such healthy debate? Yet, such contestation remains within a tightly circumscribed circle of possible positions and utterances. Academics are *not* encouraged to step back and see the PBRF from a broader philosophical and political perspective. Disputes emerge over the way the competition operates, not over whether competition should be the basis for tertiary education life in the first place.

Universities in New Zealand have a statutory obligation to serve as the 'critic and conscience of society'. Yet, of all the goals Vice-Chancellors and others in positions of power set for themselves, this would undoubtedly rank among the lowest. At best, it becomes just another bullet point buried somewhere beneath a list of 'strategic objectives'. For the most part, neither individual academics nor their leaders are held to account for failing to uphold this legal responsibility. To be sure, it is not the PBRF alone that prevents the 'critic and conscience' role being taken seriously. It can be said, however, that there is nothing in the PBRF that provides a strong incentive for committing intellectual energy to this role. To the contrary: time spent in social activism or critique will, unless this leads to measurable 'outputs' (and these must be 'quality assured'), be wasted in PBRF terms.

The PBRF, in keeping with earlier neoliberal developments in tertiary education, discourages academics from seeing the world otherwise. Alternatives can be considered but only if they are consistent with the logic Lyotard described four decades ago: the ongoing commodification of knowledge, an emphasis on performativity, and a commitment to competition. Building a counter discourse to such dominant trends will be extraordinarily difficult and will require a longer term perspective. With the PBRF now such an entrenched part of tertiary education culture in New Zealand, it is difficult to imagine research life beyond it. But policy changes over the last part of the 20th century and first part of the 21st century need to be viewed as one moment in a history of a thousand years. The university as an institution dates back to at least the Middle Ages, and arguably has its roots in even earlier times with the formation of the ancient Greek academy. Neoliberalism may be leaving a deep imprint on contemporary policy thinking, but the ideas and practices consistent with it will not remain dominant for ever.

Indeed, there have at different moments been some promising signs that neoliberalism is lessening its hold over the hearts and minds of many younger people who will become tomorrow's leaders. While the dystopian features of the academic present are clearly evident, the promise of a revival of an older spirit of utopian social reform, in a manner appropriate to the times, has by no means disappeared. The Occupy Movements that started in places such as

Wall Street in the United States and subsequently swept around the world – in Canada, the United Kingdom, Australia, and New Zealand, among other places – provided some hope that the forms of subtle control so essential to neoliberalism would not be guaranteed safe passage. The deep social divisions created by global neoliberal capitalism have spawned a new sense of shared responsibility in many quarters, including pockets of the academy. University students are among those who, as Henry Giroux (2011a) so eloquently puts it, 'tell us that the social visions embedded in casino capitalism and deeply authoritarian regimes have lost their ability to normalize their values as well as their power to intimidate and silence through threats, coercion, and state violence' (p. 12). Many of these students recognise that they have come to be seen as disposable servants of late capitalist economies. They have built up huge debts seeking the gains promised to them by higher education and they have been let down. They see the hypocrisy in politicians making cuts to public spending, while providing tax breaks for the wealthy few (Giroux, 2011b, pp. 1–2). These young people, protesting now, are in some cases the professors of the future. Similar hope might be found in the concern expressed by many in more recent years over the impact of climate change, with a determined push by those who will inherit the damaged Earth of the future to hold politicians and corporate leaders to account for their actions.

Universities have an important ongoing role to play in examining these movements, setting them in their broader historical and political contexts, and showing how they are connected to other struggles against greed and the commodification of everyday life. Researchers cannot remain neutral in the face of this push for change. Why, Giroux (2011b) asks, 'do so many academics cling to a notion of disinterested and objective scholarship and publish and make a claim to pedagogy that allegedly decries any relationship to politics, power or interest in larger social issues?' (p. 3). The answer, he says, is that 'for all intents and purposes, too many academics who make a claim to objectivity, and, in some cases, reject the presence of the military-industrial-academic complex on campus, have become irrelevant to offering any viable defense of the university as a democratic public sphere, or, for that matter, even defending to a broader public the very conditions that make their work possible' (p. 3). This is not to say that academics set out to deliberately undermine the democratic and critical ideals the university is meant to uphold; it is more a matter of such questions not being raised. Or, to be more precise, it might be said that, over time, deep immersion in a culture of commodification and performativity inhibits one's ability to truly *hear* what is being said by others. The first step, then, is to begin listening to students (p. 4). Getting involved may mean joining a protest or demonstration, but a contribution can also be made through critical teaching, 'risky' research, and a willingness to enter into dialogue with those positioned as 'Others' in neoliberal times.

A path forward lies not in attempting to return to a romanticised version of the university of the past but in acknowledging the importance of the tension between ideals and realities. This book is premised on the view that a collegial, cooperative, democratic approach to tertiary education should be preferred over the competitive, commercialised, managerialist models that have prevailed over recent decades. But it must be acknowledged that there is no simple, clear-cut contrast between different eras. The universities of old were elitist not just in an academic sense but in class terms, and only children from the most privileged families could attend. There has never been a single, 'pure' source of motivation for pursuing knowledge and undertaking research, and the 'publish or perish' phenomenon was well established before the arrival of neoliberalism and the PBRF. The PBRF has, however, systematised what was hitherto enacted in a more ad hoc way. It has made research more individualistic, more competitive, more outputs-driven than ever before. In so doing, it has reduced the idea of 'knowledge' to a shallow imitation of its former self and narrowed conceptions of what counts as worthwhile research. The PBRF, by elevating the idea of performance above all else, has dehumanised academic activity and contributed to the incremental process of turning universities into corporations.

What is needed, I believe, is a gradual but substantial shift in thinking: from the exaggerated certainties of neoliberalism and policy developments such as the PBRF to the uncertainty and questioning that has always characterised creative intellectual life; from the artificial tidiness of a well-ordered system for ranking academics as 'A', 'B', 'C', or 'R' to a more nuanced and well-rounded assessment of achievements (and then only when strictly necessary); from the logic of performance and the language of outputs to the notion of rich, complex research cultures; from the narrowness of a one-size-fits-all approach to economic and social life to a careful, open-minded consideration of alternatives; from a focus on the idea of the self-interested individual researcher to a view of academics as dialogical beings, committed to inquiry with others and to the pursuit of better worlds.

Acknowledgement

The original version of this chapter was published as Roberts, P. (2013). Academic dystopia: Knowledge, performativity and tertiary education. *The Review of Education, Pedagogy, and Cultural Studies*, 35(1), 27–43. By permission of the publisher (Taylor and Francis Group: www.tandfonline.com).

CHAPTER 3

Higher Education, Impact and the Internet

Publishing, Politics and Performativity

1 Introduction

In today's world, more scholarly material is being produced and published than ever before. Part of the explanation for this lies in the advantages conferred by the Internet in reducing space constraints and enhancing the speed of publication. Also crucial, however, is the emergence of performance-based research funding schemes and the pressures they exert on academics to publish. Drawing on examples from Britain and New Zealand, and building on the argument developed in Chapters 1 and 2, this chapter argues that such regimes can be dehumanising, fundamentally altering the way scholars think about themselves and their published work. These negative effects, it is suggested, will be exacerbated if the importance of peer review is downplayed or disregarded in favour of systems based largely or entirely on metrics. If such a scenario unfolds, the Internet could play a key role in creating more machine-like academic cultures, and intellectual life will be much the poorer for this. At the same time, the Internet could also be pivotal in allowing scholars to contest dominant practices in the assessment of published work.

2 Scholarly Publishing in the Age of the Internet

Just over two decades ago, I wrote a paper on scholarly publishing, peer review and the Internet (Roberts, 1999a). At that time, the publication of academic work in electronic form via the Internet was a relatively recent phenomenon. Indeed, the development of the Internet itself, as a vast, public digital space for communication across the globe, was still in its infancy. By the late 1980s, most academics were making use of word processors to write books and papers, but the regular use of computers for other tasks was still uncommon. By the mid-1990s, e-mail had been widely adopted and the Internet was gaining increasing prominence in scholarly life. The growth in digital technologies from that point onwards was rapid and dramatic. Where before networked computing had been largely confined to small groups serving in specialist government, military or educational roles, now the possibility of a much more open

© PETER ROBERTS, 2019 | DOI:10.1163/9789004518179_004

worldwide web emerged. For those undertaking research, the breaking down of previous barriers imposed by time and space – the idea of being able to connect almost instantly with others thousands of kilometres away – was very appealing. Within a few short years, a rich body of work emerged on the potential of the Internet to transform traditional methods of scholarly publishing.

Throughout the 1990s, there was considerable debate over a perceived 'crisis' in scholarly publishing (Astle, 1991; Greenwood, 1993; Guédon, 1994; Harnad, 1996; Odlyzko, 1994; Okerson, 1991a, 1991b; Taubes, 1996a, 1996b; Thatcher, 1995; UCSB Library Newsletter for Faculty, 1996). Print journals had become extraordinarily expensive, with annual subscription costs – typically borne by university libraries – running into the hundreds, sometimes thousands, of dollars for well-known scientific periodicals. Publication in traditional journals involved lengthy delays for academics, who would frequently have to wait at least 12 months following the acceptance of their submitted work for it to appear in print. Almost every element of the scholarly communication process was slowed down by 'print and post' systems, from submission, to reviewing, revisions, publication, and distribution. University libraries also had to find ways to store ever-growing bodies of published work, with journals combining with books, reports, and other printed materials to fill the shelves of large multi-story buildings. Finding space for everything was a perpetual problem, and many universities had to resort to using off-campus facilities to store excess academic material.

The possibility of publishing academic work electronically via the Internet seemed to offer not only a means for reducing costs, delays and storage difficulties, but also new ways to respond to the ideas and findings of scholarly peers (Arnold, 1995; Day, 1995; Harnad, 1991, 1995, 1997; Odlyzko, 1997; Okerson, 1996; Valauskas, 1997). Work could, for example, be reviewed in advance of formal submission via electronic pre-print repositories. Multiple reviewers could contribute to a networked conversation about the merits of a scholarly article or book. Ongoing, open dialogue between the author and reviewers could, in a technical sense, be easily enacted. Peer reviewers could be expected to respond more promptly than they had in the past, and authors too could communicate with editors over revisions, resubmissions, and proof-reading with greater rapidity. Web-based publication would also open up the prospect of academic work being continuously updated as new findings, critiques, or ideas emerged. There would be no single fixed and final version of a paper; instead, academic work could remain 'live' and ever-changing, appearing more as an ongoing conversation than a scholarly artefact.

In the second half of the 1990s, web-based repositories for scholarly work had started to appear. Some of these had much in common with traditional print journals, while others sought to foster new ways of presenting, distributing, reviewing, and reading academic material. As the years following the turn of the century have unfolded, the publication of research papers in digital form has continued to expand. Almost all scholarly journals are now available electronically, either via subscription-based models or on an open access basis. The case for open access in scholarly publishing has epistemological, ethical and educational foundations (Björk et al., 2010; Cope & Kalantzis, 2009; Greyson et al., 2009; Guédon, 2009; Harnad & Brody, 2004; May, 2010; Pyati, 2007) and is part of a broader trend toward greater openness in teaching, learning and research (Committee for Economic Development, 2009; Iiyoshi & Kumar, 2008; Willinsky, 2006). Enhancing access to knowledge can be seen as an important principle in a democracy, and openness, within certain limits, can be seen as a key educational virtue (Peters & Roberts, 2011).

Approaches to open access vary. Some journals charge no fees for either the submission or the reading of papers (Budapest Open Access Initiative, 2002; Suber, 2015); others, including those managed by major publishing houses such as Taylor and Francis, Elsevier, Wiley-Blackwell, and Springer, impose substantial 'author processing charges' for those who choose the open access option. These fees can range from several hundred to several thousand dollars per article. For many well-established journals, a print version of each issue is still produced, either in tandem with the electronic version or at a later date. But print copies are often only obtained by individuals if they are members of professional organisations that sponsor journals. By far the most common way to access material in journals is via library digital subscriptions. Many academic books are also now published in digital form, allowing libraries to make savings in space and the costs associated with this.

The move to digital publication for scholarly journals has, in many senses, been more seamless, less disruptive, and more conservative than might have been predicted. Access to scholarly material is now, for most faculty members and students, easier and faster than ever before. While alternative approaches to publishing keep evolving (Clarke, 2007; Morrison, 2013; Smecher, 2008; Solomon, 2002), there have, to date, been fewer changes to academic journals than some expected. Most journals retain the same key features that were evident in the print and post era, with individual articles housed together in single issues published at regular intervals. Links to other publications might be more readily enabled in some periodicals, and systems for submitting, accessing and distributing papers may have changed, but little else has altered. What *has* changed is the total amount of written material now published; this has continued to expand at a rapid rate.

Part of the explanation for this increase lies in the technical advantages associated with contemporary computing; ideas can be recorded, modified,

HIGHER EDUCATION, IMPACT AND THE INTERNET   45

formatted, and submitted for publication much more rapidly and readily than the print-based technologies of the past permitted. The Internet has also opened up new avenues and opportunities for the publication and circulation of ideas. The number of journals available in most fields of study keeps growing, with false starts and closures being far outweighed by the increase in new titles. More than this, though, the Internet has allowed for other modes of written expression via blogs and social media platforms such as Facebook and Twitter. Lines between 'scholarly' and 'popular' writing are becoming more blurred, as digital repositories open up access to material that was hitherto available only to specialists and as academics seek to gain a wider audience via other means of communication. There is also a growing academic presence on visual platforms such as YouTube. This has not been an either/or process: the increase in 'alternative' content available via the Internet has not led to a corresponding decrease in scholarly content. We may live in a world increasingly dominated by images but we are still heavily dependent on the written word, and more words are being produced, by a wider range of people, than ever before.

The opening up of opportunities for faster, easier, more accessible publication and the wider dissemination of ideas via the Internet is, however, only part of the story here. Equally important are the institutional, political and policy pressures that have been brought to bear on academics under systems of research assessment. The next section discusses one example of such a scheme: New Zealand's Performance-Based Research Fund (PBRF). Reference will also be made to Britain's Research Excellence Framework (REF). Research assessment regimes of this kind encourage a factory-like scholarly production process, with dehumanising consequences for those involved and a diminished sense of what research, publication and intellectual life have to offer. The negative consequences of such systems could be exacerbated if the principle of academic judgement via peer review is replaced with quantifiable measures of 'impact', including those generated by some of the world's most powerful Internet-based multinational companies.

3   Peer Review, Performativity and Impact

As noted in the previous chapter, New Zealand's Performance-Based Research Fund (PBRF) grew out of the work of the Tertiary Education Advisory Commission (TEAC), a body established shortly after the election of a new Labour-led government in 1999. The PBRF was introduced as part of wider suite of changes designed to advance New Zealand as a knowledge society and economy

(Ministry of Education, 2002, 2006; Roberts and Peters, 2008; TEAC, 2000, 2001a, 2001b, 2001c). It replaced a system for research funding in the tertiary sector that had, under the previous government, been based largely on student numbers. This earlier approach had created perceived injustices, with funding following the student regardless of differences in research productivity and activity between various tertiary education institutions and organisations. The PBRF would, in theory, usher in a merit-based approach to research funding, rewarding those institutions and individuals who excelled in their scholarly work (PBRF Working Group, 2002).

In making the shift to performance-based research funding, the Commission had considered examples elsewhere in the world. Britain's Research Assessment Exercise (RAE), as it was then known, was the most familiar and well-established of these. In more recent years, the RAE has morphed into what is now called the Research Excellence Framework (REF) but most of the key planks of the original scheme remain in place. The most notable of these is the principle of peer review. Under the REF, as was the case with the RAE, scholars are evaluated by disciplinary panels of their peers. Academic departments receive a grade for their research performance based on the judgements made by the relevant panel and this determines the amount of research funding. The PBRF shares much in common with the REF. Both schemes are intended to reward and encourage research achievements and contributions. New Zealand academics complete Evidence Portfolios (EPs) for a quality evaluation exercise conducted once every six years. The bulk of the PBRF funding received by participating institutions comes from the results of this assessment process, with the balance being determined by research degree completions and externally generated research income (see further, Curtis, 2008; Roberts, 2006; PBRF Review Panel, 2020; Tertiary Education Commission, 2013).

An important distinction between the REF and the PBRF, however, is that under the latter the rating is awarded to individuals, not departments. This has had a significant bearing on how researchers view themselves and their activities (Ashcroft, 2005; Middleton, 2005; Roberts, 2007a; Smith & Jesson, 2005). The REF has a number-based rating system, while the PBRF uses grades. Individual researchers in New Zealand who chose to receive their grades after the original quality evaluation, for example, learned whether they had been rated 'A', 'B', 'C', or 'R'. The first of these grades signified world-class, outstanding research achievements and contributions; the last was awarded to those whose performance was deemed inadequate to receive any PBRF funding. Minor modifications have been made to the system over the years, but the idea of awarding grades to individuals has remained. Those holding key positions of responsibility in New Zealand universities – typically, the Vice-Chancellor,

Deputy Vice-Chancellor(s), and Pro-Vice-Chancellors or Deans – may have access to the grades for PBRF-eligible academics, either across the university or in a given College or Faculty. Given this situation, individuals can experience implied or overt pressure to perform, even if they choose not to receive their grades.

The PBRF has fostered a culture of relentless production, pushing academics who may for various reasons (including heavy teaching loads or substantial service commitments) have had modest publication records to 'lift their game' as writers and researchers. Those with already impressive publishing profiles have felt compelled to keep extracting further improvements from themselves, publishing more, in better journals, and with greater recognition from peers. While many might claim that such pressures are desirable, particularly in publicly-funded institutions, the subtle effects of the PBRF on academic morale and the nature of the research activities undertaken are often overlooked. Now in New Zealand, the tendency to define oneself or others in PBRF terms can become part of the culture of everyday institutional life: 'I'm an A researcher!'; 'I'm a B now, but I'm tracking towards an A'; 'She's an Associate Professor: shouldn't she be higher than a C?'; 'I'm disposable; I'm an R'. The PBRF plays an important role in not just rewarding but also disciplining and punishing individual researchers, with an especially marked effect in subject areas such as Education where many academics have a strong professional and practitioner focus in their work (Middleton, 2005; Seddon et al., 2012; Smith & Jesson, 2005).

The language of 'outputs' dominates research discussions in universities subject to performance-based research funding, and in the end academics can begin to think of themselves in this light: *they* become 'outputs' of a system that manages and measures them and determines their worth as researchers on the basis of a six-yearly grade. As argued in the previous chapter, this dehumanises academics, reducing them, symbolically at least, to fodder in a giant revenue-generating machine. The dehumanising consequences of such regimes extend to those with whom academics work, who collectively become part of the language of outputs. Evidence portfolios in the PBRF have several components. In the 2018 quality evaluation, these included a set of four 'Nominated Research Outputs' (the publications selected by the researcher as his or her best in the evaluation period), 'Other Research Outputs' (up to 12 additional publications or presentations from within the evaluation period selected by the researcher), and 'Research Contributions' (up to 15 items that indicate the esteem in which a researcher is held by his or her peers and the contributions he or she has made to the research environment and to his or her field). Thus, to take the example of thesis supervision, rather than being seen principally as a form of teaching, service and support (cf. Roberts, 2019b), this can end up being regarded as further capital to be traded in the outputs game. Masters and Doctoral degree completions, with the required research component, attract PBRF funding, but the successes of thesis students in gaining awards or in publishing their work can also count as research contributions and form part of an academic's evidence portfolio.

The machine-like character of scholarly publishing under the PBRF and other similar schemes is, in part, a reflection of the limits imposed by time. With a six-year evaluation cycle, there is little time for sustained reading, dialogue and reflection. Time itself becomes a commodity in such a system. Time is in perpetually short supply, and the demand to produce never ceases. As discussed in the previous chapter, in the PBRF, academics are not evaluated on what they know, or on how well they can convey their knowledge to others; they are assessed for their *performance.* The language of performativity, productivity and accountability forms part of a wider, global, long-term process of progressively commodifying knowledge and reshaping universities to make them operate like corporations. This in turn reflects the broader emphasis on economic goals in shaping educational policy, a trend that has been in evidence for more than thirty years (Fitzsimons, Peters & Roberts, 1999). The PBRF, in making research a more individualistic, competitive, instrumentalist activity than ever before, is simply conforming to a pattern that has already been well established with other policy reforms in the tertiary education sector.

The PBRF might in theory be intended to reward quality over quantity, but the quality of the assessment process itself can be questioned. With its tightly prescribed word limits and its rigid evidence portfolio structure, the PBRF assessment process provides a rather restricted portrait of an individual researcher and his or her contributions. A far more well-rounded, more complex and nuanced picture might emerge in, say, appointing an academic to a senior position, where a full CV, referees' statements, a presentation, and an interview would normally be required (Roberts, 2007a). Indeed, as argued in Chapter 2, the very idea of 'quality' warrants careful interrogation. 'Quality' has become a policy buzzword, but often important questions relating to the use of this term are neglected: Quality as defined by whom? In what ways? In relation to what? Under what circumstances and in contexts? Research activities, even within one field of study, can vary so widely in their aims, methodologies and underlying theoretical assumptions that distinctions between them on the basis of 'quality' can quickly begin to seem spurious.

There is, however, one important element of the PBRF that is worth retaining in any system of research assessment: peer review. In my 1999 article I suggested that peer review would have 'a vital role to play as we move into a digital scholarly future'. It was acknowledged that '[r]efereeing may, at times,

HIGHER EDUCATION, IMPACT AND THE INTERNET

be a nasty, interest-serving exercise'; nonetheless, the benefits of peer review would 'still outweigh a situation where "anything goes"'. Given the rapid expansion in publicly available information in the age of the Internet, mechanisms for determining the rigour and integrity of online material would be essential. I noted that new systems for commenting on scholarly work were emerging (e.g., post-hoc assessments of material that has already been released, ongoing debate via interactive Internet publications, open peer review, and the updating of earlier versions of a paper to in the light of feedback from readers). Most of these systems, it was observed, 'still rely on some form of peer review as a legitimating mechanism: judgements about the quality of work are made, or sought, in the company of others with like interests and expertise'. 'This process', I concluded, 'which gives scholarly publishing its distinctive character, will be vital as the information explosion reaches full force in the electronic era' (Roberts, 1999a). Developments over the last two decades have only served to reinforce the key points made in the earlier article.

Peer review remains imperfect. It relies on a sense of trust in the fairness and competence of other scholars. Today, as in 1999, much depends on the goodwill, understanding and actions of editors. Editors exercise considerable power in determining who is selected to make judgements about the work of others and in interpreting feedback when it is received. Peer review can be conservative, as was noted in the 1999 article, and, given the veil of anonymity that still prevails in most cases, it can shield reviewers themselves from proper scrutiny about the motivations that underpin their comments. Reviewers can be slothful, arrogant, self-absorbed, narrow-minded, and mean-spirited. They can be reactionary and defensive in responding to critiques of the ideas and traditions to which they adhere. Editors may deliberately or unconsciously select reviewers who are likely to be hostile to the content or style of a submitted manuscript. They may be looking for reasons to reject a paper rather than reasons to accept it.

Despite all of these potential dangers and drawbacks with the process, peer review is still the best reassurance we have of robust and collegial judgements being made about the quality of academic work. The negative possibilities noted above exist, across different fields, but they are heavily outweighed by the positive features of peer review. Most editors and reviewers approach their duties with a strong sense of responsibility to their scholarly community. Editing and reviewing are time-consuming, difficult, often thankless tasks; they constitute a vital form of academic service. The reports completed by peer reviewers often provide constructive suggestions that demonstrably improve a submitted manuscript. Peer reviewers may notice mistakes, identify silences and weaknesses, and suggest appropriate ways for deepening and extending an argument. Thoughtful, careful reviewing of an academic article, chapter or book becomes a kind of dialogue between the author(s) and the reviewer. Peer review, at its best, continues an intellectual conversation to which a manuscript author is adding, building on work that has already been undertaken by other thinkers and researchers, allowing new insights and perspectives to emerge.

The Internet offers opportunities for making this scholarly dialogue more immediate and more sustained. This is so not just in relation to the publication of ideas but in the way evaluations are undertaken via schemes such as the PBRF and the REF. The Internet is vital, at every step in the process. A substantial majority of the work evaluated under such schemes is published via the Internet, either in scholarly journals or via reports that are made publicly available. Increasingly, books and book chapters too are available in electronic as well as hard copy form. Communication between those involved in major research projects frequently relies on the Internet. The policy documents that provide the parameters for undertaking research are also invariably available online. The Internet has aided, but not replaced, the principle of academic judgement, applied not by any one individual but in the context of a discussion among peers. Through peer review, the 'human' element of the research assessment process is retained. Peer review, particularly where this occurs via face-to-face discussion, can make the process more complicated, slower, and more expensive, but this can be seen as preferable to an approach that relies exclusively on 'big data' or automated systems for generating numbers that are taken as measures of performance.

More recently, there has been a shift from scholarly publishing *per se* to scholarly publishing with 'impact' (cf. Bruns, 2013; King's College London and Digital Science, 2015; Priem & Hemminger, 2010; Snijder, 2013). This idea is deeply problematic. It is not that academics do not want their work to have any impact; rather the problems lie in how impact is construed, interpreted and rewarded. Making a worthwhile difference in students' lives through one's teaching and research can be seen as a profoundly important way to have an 'impact' with one's work, but this is too imprecise, too ill-suited to quantitative measures of academic performance, to be seriously considered. It can take many years, sometimes decades, for the value and significance of an academic's contribution to be truly understood and appreciated by those with whom he or she works, and this does not fit well with the modus operandi for most research assessment regimes. Under the REF, care has been taken not to define 'impact' too narrowly. Nonetheless, in practice it has, internationally, become more and more closely linked with quantitative indicators such as research income and citation-based systems such as Scopus journal rankings and Google's h-index. Such trends are particularly damaging for the humanities and the social sciences, where far fewer opportunities for substantial research funding exist than in Medicine, Science, and Engineering, and where citation counts tend to be much lower than in those domains of study.

Research is becoming more heavily influenced by the language of 'metrics', an even narrower focus than the PBRF's emphasis on 'outputs'. The assumption in both cases is that if something is to count it must be measurable in some way. An independent review was recently undertaken in the UK on the role played by metrics in assessing and managing research (Wilsdon et al., 2015). In his Foreword, the Chair of the steering group responsible for the report observed:

> Metrics evoke a mixed reaction from the research community. A commitment to using data and evidence to inform decisions makes many of us sympathetic, even enthusiastic, about the prospect of granular, real-time analysis of our own activities. [...] Yet we only have to look around us, at the blunt use of metrics such as journal impact factors, h-indices and grant income targets to be reminded of the pitfalls. Some of the most precious qualities of academic culture resist simple quantification, and individual indicators can struggle to do justice to the richness and plurality of our research. (Wilsdon et al., 2015, p. III)

'Metrics', Wilsdon added, 'hold real power: they are constitutive of values, identities and livelihoods' (p. III). In making this point, Wilsdon refers to the case of Stefan Grimm, a Professor at Imperial College in London, who committed suicide in September 2014. Shortly before his death, Grimm had been informed that despite his relatively strong publication record, his research performance was inadequate: his success in gaining research funding was not at the level expected of professors in his department at Imperial. The case was widely discussed in the UK, and there are lessons for other countries in reflecting on this example.

Academics in public universities have important responsibilities to uphold if taxpayer funds are to be well spent. Undertaking rigorous research is one of those responsibilities, but there is no one best way to contribute to this key element of higher educational life. Publishing one's work in scholarly journals (or in book form) is a reasonable expectation to have of most academics, and this process has been aided in many respects by developments in the age of the Internet. It is not clear, however, why the gaining of research funding should be a universal requirement for academics, given the wide variations in readily available sources of financial support across (and even within) different fields. And even where funding is readily available, it is not self-evident that research undertaken with substantial grants is any 'better' – in terms of its rigour, its contribution to knowledge, or its potential value for others – than work completed without funding. Evaluating an academic's worth on the basis of the dollars gained through his or her research activities is another element, perhaps the ultimate step, in the broader process of dehumanisation described in this chapter and throughout this book. At first glance, it might seem odd that those charged with evaluating academic work, either through exercises such as the REF assessment or in appointment, tenure and promotion decisions, could adopt such an obviously flawed, reductionist stance in their assessment activities. Yet, as Lyotard (1984) argued in *The Postmodern Condition*, there is nothing remarkable about such an approach from a performativity point of view. In a world where knowledge is treated as just another commodity, and where the goal is to maximise outputs relative to inputs, ethical objections become irrelevant. What counts is not truth, or knowledge, but what sells. The academic world, it seems, is now firmly in the grip of this logic and unlikely to escape from it without a good deal of struggle, both within its own ranks and further afield.

New Zealand is already starting to go down the 'impact' path. A focus on impact was foreshadowed in the terms of reference for the PBRF Review Panel and reflected in the report produced by that group (PBRF Review Panel, 2020). In the New Zealand context, however, the discourse of impact may, if the recommendations of the review panel are taken up, be constructed in terms that are relevant to this country – its distinctive history and particular obligations to key groups. The PBRF Review Panel has proposed that 'Nominated Research Outputs' be replaced with a section on 'Examples of Research Excellence', to 'allow researchers to detail the research they produce, the engagement and impact relating to that research and how they support vibrant, diverse research cultures' (p. 4). The panel has recommended '[i]ncreasing the funding weighting for the subject areas of Māori Knowledge and Development and Pacific Research and for Māori and Pacific researchers' (p. 4). Importantly, the panel has also proposed that external research income be eliminated as a component of the PBRF in future rounds. If this recommendation is accepted, there may be some lessening of the pressure to evaluate one's intellectual worth in terms of dollars generated, but it must also be remembered that the PBRF is just one part of a bigger picture. The overall trend toward the quantification of academic activity will continue. External research income will still play a role in the PBRF in the way individual academics describe their contributions, and gaining large grants will still be considered a major goal in many fields of study. The tendency to equate 'bigger' (more money, larger research teams, higher citation scores, improved rankings on QS and Times Higher league tables of university performance) with 'better' will not disappear. However 'impact' is

HIGHER EDUCATION, IMPACT AND THE INTERNET 53

defined for PBRF purposes, it seems certain that broader international trends will continue to exercise considerable sway in shaping academic priorities and identities in the foreseeable future.

4   Concluding Remarks

It is unlikely that the relentless production of published work will slow down any time soon. The turn to metrics and the language of 'impact' may encourage some academics to be more strategic in their scholarly efforts – paying more attention than they may have in the past to citations and journal rankings – but it will do little to reduce the rate at which material is being published. The opening up of new forms of publication via the Internet may, if anything, contribute to an acceleration in rates of productivity. The creation of machine-like production processes, stimulated by pressures to publish under performance-based research funding schemes, is, this chapter has suggested, dehumanising. Binding measures of performance more tightly to the idea of generating revenue will make the process of dehumanisation even more marked.

The Internet could play a part in cementing these dehumanising trends but it could also be pivotal in contesting them. Internet giants such as Google, with its access to and control over vast amounts of data, can exert a powerful influence over what comes to matter in judging academic performance. The commercialisation of everyday life, aided by aggressive Internet advertising, can also leave its mark on the academic world. At the same time, the Internet can provide a platform for organising and resisting dominant structures and practices. It can enable university teachers, students and others to make links between local problems and similar concerns at a wider international level. Communication via the Internet, as a form of constructive scholarly conversation, can contribute to a stronger sense of solidarity among academics. It can enable scholars to see that what may seem like an individual matter is often something of greater collective concern.

The Internet may be increasingly dominated by corporate interests, but it still has 'unruly' tendencies that refuse to be suppressed. Academics are under pressure to publish, and their ability to determine how they publish will often be limited, but they still, in most countries at least, enjoy considerable freedom in deciding what they have to say. Paywalls put up by multinational publishing firms create some impediments in accessing 'dangerous' knowledge, yet, as this chapter has noted, there are other ways in the world of the Internet of setting ideas free. Traditional scholarly journals continue to have an important place in the academic world but there are also many other Internet-based ways to make one's views known. Being prepared to ask difficult questions will remain a key task for academics in the future, regardless of the manner in which ideas are produced, conveyed, and debated among peers.

Acknowledgement

This chapter is based on Roberts, P. (2019). Higher education, impact, and the Internet: Publishing, politics and performativity. *First Monday: The Peer-Reviewed Journal on the Internet*, *24*(5). http://dx.doi.org/10.5210/fm.v24i5.9474. With permission from the Editor (https://firstmonday.org/).

CHAPTER 4

Problematising Productivity

Neoliberalism, Wellbeing and Education

1   Introduction

Policy ideas in tertiary education can never be said to be completely dead; they have a habit, over time, of coming back to life, haunting those who wish they'd been well and truly buried. They may appear in new clothes, with different names, but their essential characteristics remain the same. In the intervening period, there will often have been important changes in the social, cultural and economic life of a country. Governments will have come and gone, crises of an economic, environmental or political kind may have emerged, and the demographic profile of a voting population may have altered. Many who encounter the latest version of an idea may have little or no memory of its earlier incarnation. Sometimes old ideas will be combined with currently fashionable policy terms ('buzzwords') to create a kind of hybrid discourse that is neither an exact duplicate of an earlier conception of reality nor a new way of seeing the world.

One example of these tendencies can be found in the New Zealand context, where ideas such as 'choice', 'flexibility' and 'innovation' have been revived, recycled and reinvented several times over the last three decades. A recent illustration of this is the work of New Zealand's 'Productivity Commission'. Over three terms in power (2008–2017) the former National government released few policy documents on tertiary education. It was left to the Productivity Commission, a body established by the government but as an independent Crown entity, to provide the only major overview of the tertiary sector during that nine-year period. With the title *New Models of Tertiary Education* (New Zealand Productivity Commission, 2017a), the Commission's 2017 report makes its intentions clear from the beginning: here, we are led to believe, we will find something different, something fresh, something forward-thinking and new. The Commission recommended a number of changes to make tertiary education more 'diverse, adaptable and responsive', with providers that are 'innovative' and of 'high quality', in the interests of creating a system that will 'meet the needs of all learners' (New Zealand Productivity Commission, 2017b, p. 1).

This chapter argues that far from being new, these ideas represent a return to a tertiary education policy discourse first popularised in the 1990s. They form part of a broader neoliberal worldview, variants of which have, as discussed in

© KONINKLIJKE BRILL NV, LEIDEN, 2022 | DOI:10.1163/9789004518179_005

previous chapters, been played out in the tertiary education sector in New Zealand and elsewhere in the world for almost thirty years. In the 1990s, there was a particular emphasis on choice and competition as key principles for tertiary education reform. These principles are revived in the Commission's report, and coupled with a discourse of innovation, flexibility and adaptability that also owes much to developments several decades ago. There is, however, a new policy 'buzzword' in the Commission's work: 'wellbeing'. This term, which is itself not new, is now being harnessed as a key element in the proposed reform of tertiary education. For the Commission, there is a close link between 'wellbeing' and 'productivity'. This, I suggest, constitutes a serious narrowing of the range of possibilities open to citizens in pursuing and achieving wellbeing, a problem that is by no means confined to New Zealand. Examples of the 'turn to wellbeing' in OECD policy discourses will also be considered. The OECD has exerted a powerful influence over policy agendas in many countries, including New Zealand. Member nations take a keen interest in their placement relative to others in the 'league tables' of economic, social and educational performance produced by the OECD, and New Zealand is no exception to this rule. Wellbeing has now become one of the yardsticks in measuring performance, reinforcing the trend, discussed in earlier chapters, toward the quantification of human experience. Seen in this light, the linking of productivity with wellbeing, while highly problematic, is also not surprising.

2   The Productivity Commission's Report: Context and Content

It has been argued throughout this book that the key features of New Zealand's current system of tertiary education can be traced back to the neoliberal economic and social restructuring process instituted in the 1980s and 1990s. In 1984, the newly-elected Labour government initiated a series of radical economic reforms. Eschewing the interventionist tendencies of the previous National government, the new Labour administration, with Prime Minister David Lange at the helm but Finance Minister Roger Douglas spearheading the changes, began to remove trade tariffs and producer subsidies, reduce regulatory controls over many industries, sell off state assets, and corporatise the public sector. Inflation was targeted, price controls were abandoned, and the New Zealand dollar was floated. These key economic changes were followed, with the return of a National government in 1990, by sweeping reforms in the social sector. Hospitals were expected to operate like businesses, welfare provisions were cut, and employers were granted greater 'flexibility' in the way they determined conditions and wages for workers. 'User pays' policies were introduced for many public services. The role of the state was, in theory, to be diminished, and more power would be placed in the hands of individuals to determine their own fate in a marketised world.

These ideas found expression in the tertiary education sector via the central constructs of 'choice' and 'competition'. Students were treated as roving 'consumers' who would make choices between competing tertiary education 'providers'. Underpinning this pivotal shift in policy discourse was a neoliberal worldview, at the heart of which was the ontology of *homo economicus*: a view of human beings as self-interested, self-contained, rational individuals who would seek to maximise their own economic advantage in a competitive world (Peters & Marshall, 1996). Decisions and actions were seen as market-style preferences. The manifestation of neoliberal ideas in institutional form was via the language, structures and practices of managerialism. Those in key positions of responsibility were recast as managers, 'performance indicators' were introduced, and a culture of academic entrepreneurialism was fostered. An ethos of competition between tertiary education providers increasingly trumped appeals to ideals such as collegiality and cooperation. Institutions sought to create their own distinctive 'brands' and devoted substantial sums of money to aggressive marketing campaigns in an effort to improve 'market share'. Further privatisation of the sector was encouraged, and in the late 1990s the number of tertiary education organisations and qualifications began to proliferate (see further, Peters & Roberts, 1999; Roberts & Peters, 2008).

Following the 1999 general election, a new Labour-Alliance coalition government was formed. One of the first policy initiatives undertaken by the government was a comprehensive review of the tertiary education sector. A Tertiary Education Advisory Commission (TEAC) was created, and four reports were produced (TEAC, 2000, 2001a, 2001b, 2001c). In a significant break from the policy process established by the National government over the preceding nine years, the Commission included several members with extensive experience as academics in the tertiary sector. Under National, policy had been largely driven by officials, with oversight and direction provided by government ministers. The TEAC reports were wide-ranging in their approach, laying out a broad vision for tertiary education as well as addressing questions relating to the organisation and funding of the sector. A theme developed by the Commissioners, and taken up by the government, was the notion of tertiary education contributing to the advancement of New Zealand as a knowledge society and economy. This theme was central to the *Tertiary Education Strategy* documents that were to follow in subsequent years (Ministry of Education, 2002, 2006). In the Labour-led years of 1999–2008, there was less emphasis on enhancing student choice and more attention to questions of inclusiveness and cohesiveness across the sector. The idea of creating a 'seamless' system, with no differentiation between providers was abandoned. The government was seen to have a clear role in steering the system and in recognising the distinctive contributions that different institutions and organisations (universities, polytechnics, wānanga, private training establishments, industry training organisations) could make to the sector.

While there were some notable differences between the two governments of 1990–1999 and 1999–2008, there were also important continuities. The idea of regarding knowledge as a commodity, promulgated under National in the 1990s, gained new momentum in the first decade of the 21st century, with initiatives to 'export' New Zealand education internationally continuing apace. There was, as discussed in previous chapters, also an intensification of competition between tertiary education providers with the development of the Performance-Based Research Fund (PBRF). Moreover, despite the best efforts of the TEAC group to cast a wider net when thinking about the purposes of a tertiary education system, economic goals continued to dominate under the Labour-led government, as they had when National was in power in the 1990s. With the return to a National government in 2008, the focus was narrowed further, with a more overt attempt to tie tertiary education tightly to the demands of employers and industry, and to the goal of enhancing economic competitiveness on the world stage. Apart from updates to the *Tertiary Education Strategy* (Ministry of Education, 2009; New Zealand Government, 2014), very little attention was paid to the sector as a whole. It wasn't until the government's third term that a more substantial document, with implications for almost every area of tertiary education policy, was produced. The document did not, however, come from the government itself but from the Productivity Commission, 'an independent Crown entity ... [that] completes in-depth inquiry reports on topics selected by the Government, carries out productivity-related research and promotes understanding of productivity issues' (New Zealand Productivity Commission, 2017a, p. 11).

In March 2017 the Productivity Commission released a report titled *New Models of Tertiary Education*. This was in response to a request from the Minister of Finance and the Minister of Tertiary Education, Skills and Employment for an inquiry framed in these terms: 'The focus ... will be on how trends, especially in technology, tuition costs, skill demand, demography and internationalisation, may drive changes in business models and delivery models in the tertiary sector' (New Zealand Productivity Commission, 2017a, p. IV). The Commission was instructed to consider 'both demand and supply factors (including market, institutional and policy constraints) relevant to the adoption of new models of tertiary education, as well as looking broadly across what new models there are or what might emerge' (p. v). The Commission's inquiry was intended to complement work being undertaken in other policy areas such as 'Skilled and Safe Work Places' and was expected to contribute to the Government's 'Business Growth Agenda' (p. vi). The final report was preceded by the release of an 'Issues Paper' in February 2016 and a draft report in September 2016 (New Zealand Productivity Commission, 2016a, 2016b). In its final form, the report is a very substantial document of over 500 pages. It provides an overview of the existing New Zealand tertiary education system, comments on outcomes and trends, and considers the need for new models of tertiary education. Extensive use is made of tables and figures to illustrate key points in the text. Reference is made to submissions on the draft version of the document and a glossary of commonly used terms is included. The completion of the final report was accompanied by a press release (New Zealand Productivity Commission, 2017b), and various responses from the government (e.g., Goldsmith, 2017a, 2017b).

The Terms of Reference provide a context for the inquiry. Issued by the Minister of Finance and the Minister for Tertiary Education, Skills and Employment, the inquiry begins from the position that while 'the tertiary education sector has adapted to significant change in the last two decades', there has also been considerable 'inertia' in the system (p. iv). Tertiary providers have demonstrated a reluctance to be 'early adopters' in moving away from traditional models (p. iv). Several key trends are identified, including continuing changes in technology, rising tuition costs, further internationalisation, new employer and student demands, and the demographic realities of an ageing and increasingly diverse New Zealand population (p. iv). Overseas providers have been 'faster and more ambitious in adapting to these trends' (p. iv) than their New Zealand counterparts. These points are reinforced in the Foreword to the report, where it is suggested that innovation has been stifled in favour of stability (pp. iii). The Commission claims that the current system of tertiary education in New Zealand 'does not adequately cater for diverse students or encourage new models to emerge to meet evolving needs and opportunities' (p. iii). There are barriers to access for some groups and the system is 'characterised by a high degree of central control', with 'increasingly prescriptive funding rules and regulatory requirements' (p. iii). The Commission wants to see greater freedom and flexibility in the system to encourage new approaches to tertiary education that will 'meet the needs of a wider variety of students' (p. iii).

Key points and recommendations are conveyed in the detailed 'Overview' provided near the beginning of the report. The Commission comments on some of the ways in which the tertiary education system has grown and changed over the last three decades. It acknowledges that New Zealand's universities rank well internationally (all are in the top 3%), that wānanga enable many students who otherwise miss out to participate in tertiary education, and that a diverse range of private training establishments can be identified (p. 1). New Zealand falls short, however, in meeting the needs of all students. The current system is too 'supply-driven', with providers too heavily focused on what the government wants. There is too much central control, with a lack of dynamism in the system, and the rules and regulations that govern the sector are too prescriptive and restrictive. The system needs to become more 'student-centred', with greater freedom and stronger incentives for providers to innovate (p. 2). The Commission recommends changes to the government's funding system to allow providers to be 'more responsive to student demand' (p. 2). Providers should be rewarded for 'good performance' in 'adding value' to students (p. 2). Enhancing student choice by offering a wider range of providers and delivery options is desirable. Introducing new models of tertiary education would improve the chances of students finding a provider that 'suits their needs and aspirations' (p. 3). The system as it is currently set up 'punishes risk-takers' (p. 3). There is a narrowness in the range of tertiary 'products' purchased by government; the sector is too homogeneous, and there are limited incentives for 'high-performing' providers to grow at the expense of 'low-performing' providers (p. 3). Quality assurance practices, instead of enabling change, have played a part in reinforcing existing practices (p. 4).

Where elsewhere in the economy government regulation plays a helpful role in limiting monopolies, in the tertiary education system the opposite is true: 'government regulations bestow market power, grant local monopolies, and require cartel structures' (p. 4). Government capping of student numbers, and a focus on younger, full-time, on-campus students, has resulted in other groups – including many prospective Māori and Pasifika students – missing out (pp. 4–5). Inflexibility is also evident in the difficulties posed by the current system for students who wish to change what they study, how and where. The system is not well prepared to cope with changing demographics in New Zealand society or with the demands created by technology for new skills. Predicting future trends and assessing their influence on tertiary education is difficult, and what is needed is a system that can respond more rapidly, spontaneously and easily to whatever changes do occur (p. 5). Tertiary education involves 'co-production' and this works best when 'providers and consumers have shared objectives' (p. 6). Students need to be better prepared to make decisions about their own tertiary education. This will require, among other things, improvements in the way career services are provided for young people in schools.

Better systems of credit transfer need to be available to ease the process of mixing and matching courses from different providers (p. 6).

The Commission recommends that providers with 'a strong record of educational performance' be granted self-accrediting status (p. 7). The current process of collective accreditation tends to be too conservative (defining quality according to existing practices), stifling innovation. Rather than being tied to full-time study, funding should be available on a more flexible basis. Polytechnics and institutes of technology should be able to deliver education anywhere in New Zealand without the approval of the Tertiary Education Commission. The current imbalance in the way research and teaching are treated also needs to be addressed. The Productivity Commission claims that in universities academic success is presently much more dependent on research performance than teaching performance. Changes need to be made to better reward teaching performance, and the legal requirement that degrees are mainly taught by those engaged in research should be removed.

Tertiary education institutions that can demonstrate financial competence should, the report suggests, be given responsibility to manage their own assets and debts, and should not be exempt from paying local government rates. With greater institutional autonomy and responsibility of this kind, tertiary education institutions will be better able to 'direct capital investments towards new models of education' (p. 7). The system should also allow 'new entrants' into the tertiary education market, including those from overseas. To date, the attention paid to this area has often been negative – with a focus on the low quality of the education provided by new entrants – but it needs to be noted that 'the beneficiaries are people who were previously not accessing the product or service at all' (p. 8). The report also recommends that the Student Loan Scheme should be extended to courses approved by NZQA but not subsidised by the Tertiary Education Commission. Greater flexibility in allowing institutions to raise fees on some courses should be permitted. Funding should follow student demand. Providers should be given incentives to continually improve their performance in 'adding value' to students (p. 8). Funding for courses should be determined by their 'credit value', rather than relying on the assumption that all students proceed at the same pace in their learning (p. 8). Responsibility for managing and monitoring the Crown's 'ownership interest' should rest with Treasury, not with the Ministry of Education and the Tertiary Education Commission (p. 8). Finally, a new Tertiary Education Strategy should be developed, with goals to be measured by an 'indicator framework' that will 'populate the accountability documents of education agencies, in line with their respective roles and responsibilities' (p. 9).

62   CHAPTER 4

3   A Critique

The Productivity Commission's revival of choice and competition as key elements of the tertiary education system is premised on the same ontology of *homo economicus* that dominated earlier neoliberal policy agendas. The world envisaged by the Commission is one populated by discrete, self-contained, rational individuals, making continuous consumer-style choices. Choices will, it seems, be driven primarily by self-interest. It is assumed that individuals want to exercise a certain kind of freedom through the act of choosing, but the nature of that act – i.e., the process of choosing – is given little attention. It is acknowledged that further guidance may need to be provided through careers advice in schools to better prepare students for their choice-making activities at a tertiary level. But the concept of choice itself is not interrogated, nor is its inherent value questioned. There is little recognition of the ways in which we are shaped by social, political and cultural structures, policies and practices. In the Commission's report, there is, in short, nothing that resembles what might be called the 'political economy' of tertiary education. This is a fundamental weakness that was also clearly evident in the neoliberal reforms of the 1990s.

Consumer-style preferences do not emerge out of nowhere; they are heavily influenced, for example, by powerful multinational corporations. For students in the 21st century, social media giants exercise a particularly notable sway over the development of wants and worldviews, but they are but one part of larger picture. Developing the ability to critically examine one's choices, not merely make them, is arguably a key goal of tertiary education. Learning how to place thoughts, feelings, decisions, and actions in a larger context is crucial if students are to emerge from tertiary education institutions not just as consumers and competitors but as thoughtful, responsible citizens. In the Commission's report, education is seen not as a process of formation but as a transaction. The idea of committing to a process that could be unsettling and uncomfortable – a process that could be utterly transformative, changing one's view of oneself and the world – seems a world away from the portrait painted by the Productivity Commission. For the Commission, education is not so much something to be experienced or encountered, as a radical challenge to one's existing perception of reality; rather, it is merely something to be purchased, as a means to an economically advantageous end.

No serious consideration is given to the possibility that in some circumstances, it may be desirable to restrict the scope for choice. Such restrictions can be readily defended on the basis that they are often necessary if students are to acquire the knowledge and experience necessary to make better choices later in life. 'Compulsion' now appears to be a dirty word, but it has an important role to play in developing academic readiness and in providing a platform for enhancing both breadth and depth in understanding. Restrictions on the number of tertiary education institutions and organisations can also be justified, with a compelling case to be made, in a country as small as New Zealand, for fewer institutions doing what they do well rather than multiple providers (public and private) competing aggressively against each other in the same areas of study. The rapid and dramatic proliferation of new qualifications and providers was, again, a legacy of the neoliberal policies of the 1990s. It should be noted, however, that this process continued for several years into the 21st century, before an attempt was made by the then Labour-led government to bring greater coherence to the system, with a recognition that different institutions – universities, polytechnics, and wānanga, for example – each have something distinctive to offer, and that excessive duplication and competition are undesirable. The Commission's recommendations signal a return, with some caveats, to the notion of relatively unfettered expansion of the tertiary education market.

Much is made of the point that we live in rapidly changing world. If we are to thrive in this world, the Commission suggests, we will need to be flexible, innovative and entrepreneurial. These ideas are, like the notions of choice and competition, reminiscent of a discourse first promoted by New Zealand politicians and policy-makers in the 1990s. The whole tertiary education system, the Productivity Commission implies, needs to operate in a much more market-like manner, with a host of different 'providers' being granted the liberty to sell their 'products' to 'consumers', with few constraints on what is taught, how or by whom. Tertiary education institutions and organisations should, more than anything else, be governed by *what students want*, and should be ever ready to adapt in meeting changing demands. Government involvement in the sector should be minimised, with a focus not on providing a sense of purpose and direction for tertiary education but on reducing barriers to competition. What the sector becomes – i.e. what subjects tend to be favoured, and how they are taught – should largely be left to the market to decide. Quality assurance requirements need to be loosened, and there should be greater scope for innovation to be rewarded. Those who are performing well should flourish, and the market will supply the appropriate corrective mechanisms to punish those who fail to provide what students want. Too much power has been invested in the hands of institutions and organisations; the system has been subject to what was, in the past, referred to as 'provider capture'. The balance of power needs to be shifted back towards the 'consumers' of tertiary education, who are assumed, with a little help from careers advisors, to know what they need and how best to choose between competing providers.

In the Commission's report, knowledge is conceived as a commodity, with an exchange value. It is sold by tertiary education providers and purchased by student consumers, who can, in turn, trade what they learn for employment and advancement. This construction of knowledge is consistent with the trends identified by Lyotard (1984) in *The Postmodern Condition*, and the principle of performativity discussed in that work also prevails here. The tertiary education system is regarded by the Commission as unacceptably cumbersome and too slow to change. It is heavily bureaucratic and mired by too many regulatory constraints. It is, overall, considerably less efficient and effective than it should be in meeting the variety of actual and potential student demands. The language of 'performance' leaves an indelible mark on the report, and the idea of seeking to extract continual improvements through greater efficiencies in the system (maximising outputs relative to inputs) is taken as a given. The value of research in deepening and extending knowledge and understanding, for both teachers and learners, is undermined. The Commission reprises a move first made in the 1990s to break down alleged barriers between institutions, according no special status to degrees among the suite of different qualifications on offer in the tertiary education marketplace. In a system where free enterprise is favoured, with a market populated not just by competing local providers but international profit-driven players as well, the longstanding statutory requirement that degrees be mainly taught by those active in research no longer makes sense. 'Knowledge' becomes whatever those selling it say it is. Indeed, there is seldom a need, in the ideal system envisaged by the Productivity Commission, for knowledge to be mentioned at all. Performance, as measured by efficiency and effectiveness in meeting student demands, is what matters, and the need for either academic staff or students to show what they know becomes less important.

The Commission's aim is to 'provide insightful, well-informed and accessible advice that leads to the best possible improvement in the wellbeing of New Zealanders' (New Zealand Productivity Commission, 2017, p. 11). The tag line employed on the Commission's website at the time the report on tertiary education was released makes the nature of the goal more explicit: 'Productivity Growth for Maximum Wellbeing'. This gives a clear indication of how wellbeing is conceived, as one element in a broader neoliberal narrative. Wellbeing is tied, both directly and indirectly, to economic advancement. Being productive, it is assumed, will lead to greater individual happiness and better social outcomes for the country as a whole. It is important to note that productivity in this context does not mean 'being productive' in any number of different spheres of life – for example, in 'producing' healthy vegetables, or in having a 'productive' conversation – but rather refers, quite specifically, to productivity in commercial terms. To be productive is to be efficient in generating wealth, either for oneself or for others; it is to 'perform' in a certain way, in a market system. There is no reflexive acknowledgement in the report of this narrowness. Alternative conceptions of productivity are not explored; nor is there any questioning of the merits of making this a primary goal for all New Zealanders. Part of the role of tertiary education might be to encounter ideas that are *un*productive: to consider thinkers and theories that do not have to lead anywhere beyond themselves. Tertiary education should encourage students to ask questions of notions such as productivity, and should enhance the ability to think critically about the dominant discourses and practices that structure our lives. Being 'unproductive' for a few years in one's life, with a chance to read and reflect and discuss, can be seen as time well spent, given the influence such experiences can have on our formation as responsible, well-rounded, reflective citizens.

The emergence of 'wellbeing' as a theme in policy discourse is by no means confined to the Productivity Commission. The linking of productivity with wellbeing may seem odd, but this is merely an extension of the explicit emphasis on economic advancement favoured by the National government of 2008–2017. Making New Zealanders more productive was seen as essential for the country's future prosperity, and wellbeing was assumed to be closely tied to prosperity. With a Labour government now in power, references to wellbeing have not disappeared; to the contrary, they now seem to be everywhere. 'Wellbeing' has become a 'hot topic', not just in official government policy but also in institutions such as schools and universities. New Zealand has a 'Wellbeing Budget', and it is no longer sufficient to talk of balancing a single financial bottom line. Economic policy, as well as social policy, is expected to be consistent with the overarching goal of enhancing wellbeing. Reducing child poverty, providing more social housing, and improving services for those suffering from mental health difficulties have all been seen as government priorities. Some attention has also been paid to the notion of caring for the environment. The global Covid-19 pandemic has only served to heighten this awareness of the need to attend to the wellbeing of New Zealand citizens. The possibility of rising rates of domestic violence in homes during periods of lockdown has been noted. The potential distress created for employers and employees by dramatic drops in business has also been recognised. The government has responded with subsidies and pay-outs, amounting to tens of billions of dollars in total, but there has also been an admission that not all businesses will be able to be saved.

The rise of 'wellbeing' as a prominent theme in policy development is evident elsewhere in the world as well. Key international organisations such as the OECD have led the charge in bringing the 'wellbeing' motif more to the fore in policy thinking, with flow-on effects for member states. In 2013, the OECD issued a 270-page document setting out guidelines for measuring 'subjective well-being', which was defined as '[g]ood mental states, including all of the various evaluations, positive and negative, that people make of their lives, and the affective reactions of people to their experiences' (OECD, 2013, p. 29). The stated intention was to provide a broad and inclusive definition but not a 'hopelessly vague concept' (p. 29). There is, it is claimed, 'general agreement among experts on the specific aspects that comprise subjective well-being' (p. 29). It is noted that the measurement of subjective wellbeing is often conflated with the measurement of 'happiness', but this, it is asserted, is 'both technically incorrect (there is more to subjective well-being than happiness) and misleading' (pp. 28–29). Equating the two 'lends support to sceptics who characterise the measurement of subjective well-being in general as little more than "happiology"' (p. 29). The OECD's approach goes beyond this, adhering to the widely held view that a distinction must be drawn between 'a cognitive evaluation of the respondent's life as a whole (or aspects of it)' and 'measures of affect, which capture the feelings experienced at a particular point in time' (p. 29). The OECD also recognises that there is a 'clear eudaimonic aspect of subjective well-being, reflecting people's sense of purpose and engagement' (p. 29). Eudaimonia is taken to mean 'psychological flourishing' (p. 29). Incorporating each of these three dimensions subjective wellbeing (life evaluation, affect and eudaimonia), the OECD identifies several core measures of subjective wellbeing. The highest priority in determining these core measures is 'international comparability'; these are measures 'for which there is the most evidence of validity and relevance, for which the results are best understood, and for which policy uses are most developed' (p. 140).

The 2013 document on measuring subjective wellbeing is one part of the larger 'OECD Better Life Initiative'. Under this heading, the OECD has issued a series of papers, presentations and reports, some of which have been generated by surveys of wellbeing in member nations. The Better Life Initiative has three core elements: 'Building a better evidence base for policy', 'Developing better measures of people's well-being', and 'Stimulating debate and reaching out to broad audiences' (OECD Better Life Initiative, 2019, p. 1). The OECD identifies four important features of its approach to measuring wellbeing: 'It puts people (individuals and households) at the centre of the assessment'; 'It focuses on well-being outcomes – i.e. aspects of life that are directly and intrinsically important to people, rather than the inputs and outputs that might be used to deliver those outcomes'; 'It considers the distribution of outcomes across the population as an important feature shaping the well-being of societies, including disparities associated with age, gender, education and income'; and 'It features both objective and subjective data, recognising that to understand people's well-being you need to know both their objective circumstances and how they feel about their lives' (p. 2). (See further, Balestra, Boarini, and Tosetto, 2018.) From 2011 to 2017, four reports on data gathered from member countries were released. The 2017 edition of *How's Life?* (the title used for this series of reports) included results from 36 member nations and 5 additional partner countries. The report 'presents the latest evidence from over 50 indicators, covering both current well-being outcomes and the resources (natural, human, social and economic capitals) that contribute to sustaining well-being over time' (p. 5). The specific indicators are grouped together under a number of broader dimensions of wellbeing: 'income and wealth', 'jobs and earnings', 'housing conditions', 'work-life balance', 'health status', 'education and skills', 'social connections', 'civic engagement', 'environmental quality', 'personal security', and 'subjective well-being' (OECD Better Life Initiative, 2017, p. 2). In the surveys of each country, an indication of improvement, deterioration or no/little change is provided in relation to each of these dimensions, from one measuring point to the next (for most countries in the 2017 report, the comparison was between 2005 and 2015/2016) (p. 2).

The OECD has also taken an international lead in linking wellbeing with productivity. Pre-dating the release of the New Zealand Productivity Commission's 2017 report on tertiary education by two years, the OECD issued a substantial document titled *The Innovation Imperative: Contributing to Productivity, Growth and Well-being* (OECD, 2015). The OECD claims that 'innovative economies are more productive, more resilient, more adaptable to change and better able to support higher living standards'. Innovation, it is suggested, can enable people to lead better, more prosperous lives (p. 3). Innovative societies are built on characteristics such as following: a 'skilled workforce', a 'sound business environment', a 'strong and efficient system for knowledge creation and diffusion', '[p]olicies that encourage innovation and entrepreneurial activity', and a 'strong focus on governance and implementation' (p. 12). Innovation, it is argued, 'matters not only for growth, but also for health, the environment and a range of other policy objectives that are related to well-being' (p. 17). It is recognised that innovation can sometimes lead to unemployment, which can impact negatively on wellbeing. This is why government incentives and initiatives to support innovation need to be seen as part of a wider policy tool box. Innovation can, however, also play an important role in 'inclusive growth' (p. 23), an approach to economic development built on the principle of sharing 'the benefits of prosperity more evenly across social groups' (p. 23). It is acknowledged that in 'high-income countries and emerging market economies, ... income inequality has reached levels unprecedented in the post-war period' (p. 23). Innovation needs to be harnessed in ways that will contribute to a reduction in inequalities, and not just of a financial kind, for '[i]nequalities in other non-income outcomes, including educational attainment, health conditions and employment opportunities, are also increasingly recognised as influencing not only well-being, but also growth' (p. 23).

The current New Zealand government's development of a 'Wellbeing Budget' echoes a call from the OECD to build an 'economy of well-being' (Gurría, 2019). An economy of this kind creates a 'virtuous circle' in which the wellbeing of citizens 'drives economic prosperity, stability and resilience'; at the same time, those 'good macroeconomic outcomes' help to 'sustain well-being investments over time' (p. 2). In many respects, however, there is a closer connection between the OECD's statements and those made by the Productivity Commission under the previous National government. In more recent times, with the emergence of the global Covid-19 pandemic, discourses on wellbeing have continued to evolve. Talk of productivity has taken a backseat to the more pressing concerns of staying alive and healthy in the face of alarming death rates from the virus around the world. With the emergency measures put in place during the crisis, New Zealand's Prime Minister, Jacinda Ardern, has fashioned a new language of 'kindness' that hitherto would have seemed unusual in political discourse. Urging citizens to be kind to each other, as Prime Minister Ardern did repeatedly in 2020, shifts the focus away from the economy toward the realm of social relations. This discourse is not just about being well oneself; it is also concerned with attending to the wellbeing of others. Uttering such words from a press conference podium does not, of course, mean they will be embraced or taken up by all citizens. But there is something of a departure here, in the rhetoric at least, from the notion that wellbeing has a close connection with advantaging oneself over others in financial terms. The underlying ontology also moves away from a focus on the individual, and the pursuit of individual self-interest in particular, to an understanding of humans as social beings – as necessarily connected with each other. There is an implicit recognition now, even if this is not explored explicitly in policy, that our thoughts and feelings, our aspirations and goals, our identities, are shaped through our relations with others, our day-to-day cultural practices, and our participation in social institutions.

The political rhetoric may have shifted, but the larger canvas on which the picture of wellbeing is painted has not. The Productivity Commission, the OECD, and the current New Zealand government all take neoliberal global capitalism, in one variation or another, as a given in shaping policy agendas. The Covid-19 crisis, like the global financial crisis of 2008–09, has done little to disrupt the underlying ethos of consumption that drives contemporary economies. In perilous times, citizens are not urged to radically reassess their current wants and past patterns of consumption but to start spending again. The OECD recognises the need to go beyond GDP in determining national and international goals (see Cavalletti & Corsi, 2018), but economic growth is still seen as fundamentally important. Economic growth in the contemporary capitalist world relies heavily on the principle of competition, and this takes place not on an 'even playing field' but under conditions more advantageous to some (countries, corporations and individuals) than others. Inequalities of the kind identified in OECD reports are not a distortion of capitalism as a mode of production but completely consistent with it. Taking not just GDP but also wellbeing into account in developing policy may, over time, reduce these inequalities but the capitalist system will always 'fight back' against such changes. Appeals to wellbeing in a global economic environment structured by ruthless competition, with tech giants fighting for ever greater control over citizens' minds as well as wallets, will be a moderating influence at best. More cynically, it might be argued that wellbeing has been harnessed to support the perpetuation of the capitalist machine. Keeping citizens 'happy', and/or 'well' in other ways, is *good* for capitalism. The rise of 'wellbeing' as a key policy buzzword has coincided with the period immediately following the global financial crisis, when widespread concern was expressed, via the 'Occupy' movement and other forms of protest, over the '1%' – the concentration of a grossly disproportionate share of the world's wealth in the hands of very few people. In earlier decades, references were made to the need to maintain a certain level of 'social cohesion' in market economies to avoid excessive social disruption to 'business as usual' (see Roberts & Peters, 2008). 'Wellbeing' now seems to play a similar role. By keeping people 'well', or making them *feel* as if they are being kept well, governments, corporations and international organisations also make them more productive, more efficient, more accepting of the world as it is.

There are also searching philosophical questions that can be posed when considering wellbeing. These have particular relevance to tertiary education. The OECD has attempted to distance itself, almost in a defensive manner, from the simple equating of 'subjective wellbeing' with 'happiness', but the connections between these two ideals are undeniable. 'Subjective wellbeing' emerged from work on happiness conducted by 'positive psychologists' who wished to offer a corrective to what they saw as an unbalanced focus on the negative (disease, disorders, and so on) in their field. Positive psychology has also played a role in reconfiguring the language of happiness (see, for example, Seligman, 2002). In the past, those interested in exploring conceptions of happiness might have turned to philosophers for answers, and would have found much of substance in pursuing these inquiries. In the West alone, there is a long history of thought on this topic, dating back to Plato, Aristotle and other ancient Greek philosophers. Over the last two decades, however, there has been a paradigmatic shift in the way happiness is understood. We have witnessed the emergence of new discourses on the so-called 'science' of happiness (e.g., Layard, 2005). With this has come the corresponding idea that happiness can, and should, be 'measured'. The OECD may have moved away from the narrower notion of happiness to the more expansive idea of wellbeing, but a similar scientist and performative logic has been applied to the latter term. The OECD regards the measurement of wellbeing as not only possible but highly desirable. With data on measures of wellbeing gathered from dozens of countries, a kind of competition is established between nations over their performances on wellbeing league tables. Discourses on wellbeing thus play a part, and not an insignificant one, in reinforcing the view that value can best be determined through competing and comparing.

'Subjective wellbeing' has increasingly been converted, by politicians, corporations and international organisations, into the more general construct of 'wellbeing', and, with that transition, has become a powerful means for imparting a positive spin to policies that might otherwise be less appealing. There is an extensive critical literature on happiness, wellbeing, and the assumptions underpinning work in positive psychology, and educationists have made a significant contribution to this body of work.[1] At the most basic level, almost all utterances about wellbeing assume that 'happiness' is desirable, and that 'unhappiness' should be minimised or avoided. Even if this much will not be admitted, it will invariably be taken as given that being 'well' is preferable to being 'unwell'. But these ideas do not need to be so readily accepted. Suffering is an important part of many lives, and can take many different forms. The tendency to want to avoid suffering at all costs, in order to quickly restore happiness or to be 'well', can distract us from examining painful experiences more closely. Appeals to wellbeing can have the effect of 'killing off' debate: Who could possibly object to the idea that we should seek to be well and want this for others? Part of the problem here is the binary logic implied by much of the thinking on wellbeing; one is either 'well' or 'not well'. The tendency to speak and act as if wellbeing and happiness are politically neutral terms is also troubling; such notions need to be contextualised. We need to ask ourselves where they have come from, who is promoting them, and why. Happiness and wellbeing are, in the contemporary capitalist world, 'big business'. Hundreds of millions of dollars are generated every year for those selling products and services ostensibly devoted to improving wellbeing or making people happier. There is a lucrative market for prescription drugs designed to lift moods and enhance subjective wellbeing. There are self-help books, wellness retreats, and 'life coaches'. There is, in short, a substantial 'happiness industry', and this continues to flourish with the transition to the broader notion of wellbeing.

Those who profit from the current obsession with wellbeing also play a part in affirming other dominant patterns of thought. Being 'positive' and/or 'optimistic', for example, will generally be cast in a more favourable light than being 'negative' and/or 'pessimistic'. There is, at times, a sense of moral superiority associated with efforts to promote wellbeing. But there is a rich, complex, well-established body of philosophical work that calls some of these comfortable assumptions into question. Pessimistic and existentialist currents of thought date back hundreds of years, and the thinkers in those traditions raise important questions about happiness, suffering and despair relevant to current discourses on education and wellbeing.[2] Philosophers and novelists such as Kierkegaard, Dostoevsky, Schopenhauer, Unamuno, Weil, Camus, and Beauvoir, among others, show that suffering, unhappiness and despair can play a significant role in our formation as human beings. Acknowledging that suffering occurs, and taking the time to reflect on it, can be an educative experience. Distinguishing between different forms of suffering is important here. Where people are starving, homeless, or in great pain, every effort should, of course, be made to address their suffering. Learning from suffering is not the same as endorsing it, let alone actively promoting it. But when attention is paid to the forms of intellectual and emotional development we seek to encourage through our educational endeavours, the situation is not so clear-cut.

A case can be made to suggest that tertiary education should, in some respects, make students 'unhappy'; it should unsettle them, make them uncomfortable, a little 'on edge'. Tertiary education should not be concerned with simply offering choices, via competing providers, among different 'products', as the Productivity Commission would put it. It should offer the opportunity to have our most cherished assumptions rendered problematic; it should prod us to probe further. It should expand our horizons for inquiry, and open our minds to new ways of looking at human beings and the world. An educational experience at this level of study should challenge us and transform us; it should be a life-changing process. While undergoing the forms of learning associated with such a process, students can be both 'well' and 'unwell'. They may enhance their capacity for critical thought, and this attribute can be seen as desirable in any 'healthy' democracy. But the formation of a critical consciousness also means that students inner lives will become more difficult in some ways, more complicated and demanding, with ethical dilemmas now to be addressed that might in the past never have arisen. Consciousness can, as Unamuno (1972) saw it, become a kind of 'disease', but one we must learn to accommodate and live with.

72 CHAPTER 4

One final point is worth noting when considering the insertion of 'wellbeing' into policy discourses: there is, in the reports produced by bodies such as the Productivity Commission and the OECD, a revealing absence of any robust theory of oppression. On the face of it, this might seem surprising, for some of the challenges to wellbeing identified by the OCED appear to lend themselves well to framing in those terms. Problems relating to poverty, crime, malnutrition, access to safe drinking water, and the availability of health services, for example, can all be understood as symptoms of a deeply oppressive social order. The language of oppression is, however, perhaps seen as too politically charged for the work undertaken by an organisation such as the OECD. Yet, it may be exactly what is needed if the problems are to be truly understood. Other similarly charged words, such as 'exploitation' and 'liberation', also seldom appear. There is no neutral turf to stand on here, and silences on questions relating to oppression speak volumes about the politics at work in discussions of wellbeing by governments, officials and international agencies. Wellbeing, as a 'safer', less 'loaded' term, can provide a kind of shield or smokescreen, inhibiting the digging below the surface that might be necessary if conversations about these matters are to lead to lasting, meaningful change for oppressed groups around the world.

4 Conclusion

New Zealand's Productivity Commission offers analysis and advice for the New Zealand government on a wide range of different areas of economic and social policy. Its report on tertiary education in 2017 was substantial and must be acknowledged for its contribution to ongoing discussion in this area. This chapter has argued, however, that while looking to the future, the report also looks to the past, adopting, in a largely uncritical fashion, key ideas from the neoliberal policies of the 1990s. To the familiar mix of choice, competition, innovation, and flexibility, the Commission adds the notion of 'wellbeing'. This too owes something to the past, albeit the more recent past, mirroring other applications of this term by international organisations and governments around the world. Among the most influential of these bodies is the OECD, where, under the auspices of its *Better Life* initiative, wellbeing has been adopted as a major theme in comparing member nations. Wellbeing has, however, been too tightly wedded to the ideas of prosperity, performance and productivity, and has been harnessed to tacitly reinforce the continuation of neoliberal, global capitalism as the dominant mode of production across the world. Tertiary education can and should play a role in questioning the status quo, in problematising established patterns of life. Study in universities and other tertiary institutions should create a certain discomfort, and in that sense, complicate the picture of wellbeing painted for us by bodies such as the Productivity Commission and the OECD. Tertiary education can make us 'unhappy', but in doing so, it can also lead, in the longer term, to genuine, substantial change, both at a personal level and on a wider national and global scale.

Notes

1   Compare, Binkley (2011); Cigman (2012, 2014); Ecclestone (2011); Ecclestone and Hayes (2008); Elwick and Cannizzaro (2017); Ferguson (2007); Gibbs (2015, 2017); Gibbs and Dean (2014); Guilherme and de Freitas (2017); Jackson and Bingham (2018); Miller (2008); Rappleye et al. (2020); Reveley (2016); Roberts (2016); Shaw and Taplin (2007); Skea (2017); Spratt (2017); Suissa (2008); Wilson (2008); Zembylas (2020).
2   For a helpful discussion of the pessimistic tradition, see Dienstag (2006). The relevance of existentialist thought for education is demonstrated by Webster (2009). On the educational and ethical significance of suffering, see Carusi (2017); Chen (2011, 2016); Jardine, McCaffrey and Gilham (2014); McKnight (2010); Mintz (2013); Ozolins (2003); Roberts (2016).

CHAPTER 5

'It Was the Best of Times, It Was the Worst of Times ...'

Philosophy of Education in the Contemporary World

1　Introduction

'It was the best of times, it was the worst of times ...': so begins Charles Dickens' classic novel, *A Tale of Two Cities* (Dickens, 2003, p. 5). A similar assessment might be made of philosophy of education in our current age. In some senses, this is a moment of crisis for the field: few academic positions are available, there is little or no substantial philosophical content in most teacher education programmes, and theoretical work is under attack from many who favour more narrowly instrumentalist approaches to teaching and learning. At the same time, there are signs of great hope: key journals in which philosophers of education publish are flourishing, many new areas of inquiry have opened up, and, in some parts of the world, significant numbers of talented and enthusiastic doctoral students are completing philosophical theses in Education. This chapter reflects on this state of affairs and ponders possible futures for philosophy of education. It fleshes out elements of the argument touched on only briefly in earlier chapters. Thus far, the focus has been mainly on how the logic of performativity has impacted on tertiary education and research policy. Consideration has been given to the implications of neoliberal policy changes for academics in general. Here, more direct attention is paid to what working in the neoliberal era has meant for one community of scholars in particular: philosophers of education. Developments in the Philosophy of Education Society of Australasia (PESA) are examined as part of a broader international picture. Drawing on the work of Pierre Hadot (1995), I also consider what it might mean to talk of philosophy of education as *a way of life* in the contemporary world.

2　Shifting Sands: The Evolution of PESA

It is a common refrain that philosophy of education enjoyed its heyday about two generations ago. Accounts vary, but most locate this period of relative intellectual prosperity somewhere in the years between the early 1960s and the late 1970s (Clark, 2006, 2011; M. A. Peters, 2009a; Snook, 2009; Wilson, 2003).

© SPRINGER SCIENCE+BUSINESS MEDIA, 2013 | DOI:10.1163/9789004518179_006

The appointment of R.S. Peters to a chair in philosophy of education at the Institute of Education in the University of London in 1962 is usually noted as a significant milestone in the development of the field. Peters had come from a background in philosophy and psychology and had already made some important contributions in those domains before turning his attention to education. In collaboration with Paul Hirst, R.F. Dearden, and others, he built what became known as the 'London School' of analytic philosophy of education (Dearden, Hirst & Peters, 1972; Hirst, 1974; Hirst & Peters, 1970; R. S. Peters, 1970, 1973). This was an approach to educational questions centred on the rigorous analysis of concepts. Peters investigated, in close analytical detail, what we might mean when we speak of 'education' and 'the educated man'; others paid careful attention to indoctrination, teaching and schooling. The focus for Peters was on the way we use such concepts in our 'ordinary language'. It is clear that analytic philosophers of education were indebted to the later Wittgenstein but the extent to which they remained faithful to his ideas is a matter for some debate (M. A. Peters, 2009a, p. 803).

PESA emerged and grew as this body of work was making its mark in educational circles. Bill Andersen (2009), a founding member, recalls that after spending two years studying under Peters in 1967 and 1968 he returned to the University of Sydney determined to establish a society for philosophy of education similar to the one already in place in Britain. Preliminary work was undertaken in 1969, and in 1970, with an inaugural conference at the University of New South Wales, the Society that had started informally the previous year formally came into being (p. 738). In the minutes of the 1970 gathering the original name considered for the new organisation – 'The Australasian Philosophy of Education Society' – was crossed out and replaced with 'The Philosophy of Education Society of Australasia' (Haynes, 2009, p. 738), thereby sparing future members the ribbing of colleagues who might label them 'APES'. Peters had visited Australia and New Zealand in 1969, and in 1972 he enjoyed a productive term on leave at the University of Canterbury. Both Peters and Hirst served as speakers at PESA conferences, the former in 1972 and the latter in 1976 (Snook, 2009). The first meeting of the new Society was attended by 15 people and in the years that followed membership grew rapidly, reaching 115 by 1974 (Haynes, 2009, p. 738). By 1976, branches had been established in four Australian centres (Sydney, Melbourne, Adelaide, and Perth) and two New Zealand cities (Auckland and Christchurch) (p. 739).

While the influence of the London School and Peters in particular was undeniable, PESA had, from the beginning, included members with other backgrounds and interests. The tradition of American pragmatism, and especially the work of Dewey, has always been present in PESA's history (Marshall, 1987;

76   CHAPTER 5

M. A. Peters, 2009b, p. 737), and from the mid-1970s Australasian philosophers of education were to the fore in mounting a Marxist critique of Peters. Kevin Harris's paper, 'Peters on Schooling', presented at the 1976 conference, was especially noteworthy in this respect (see Harris, 2009; Snook, 2009; Walker, 2009). Other Sydney-based scholars, including James Walker and Michael Matthews, were also prominent in offering an alternative to Peters and Hirst. The link to the United States as well as Britain was strong, not only via the seminal published works of Dewey (1910, 1966, 1997), Scheffler (1960, 1973) and others, but also through institutional connections. Several members active in PESA in the 1970s and 1980s had undertaken doctoral study at the University of Illinois in Urbana-Champaign (Ivan Snook, Bruce Haynes, Felicity Haynes, Brian Hill, and Graham Oliver). In later years, a number of New Zealanders and Australians were to move to Urbana-Champaign as Faculty appointees, among them several who have contributed significantly to philosophy of education (Michael Peters, Fazal Rizvi and Tina Besley). The intellectual currents that informed PESA discussions in the 1970s and early 1980s also included existentialism (Vandenberg, 2009), the 'subversive' work of Paulo Freire, Ivan Illich, Everett Reimer, and Postman and Weingartner (Harris, 2009; M. A. Peters, 2009a, 2009b), theological anthropology and ethics (Andersen, 2009; Hill, 2009), and Quinean physicalism (Clark, 2006; Evers, 2009; Walker, 2009), among other influences.

From the mid-1980s to the early 2000s, the fortunes of the Society waxed and waned but the consensus among most Australasian commentators appears to be that by comparison with the 1970s, this was a period of relative decline (Clark, 2006; Haynes, 2009; M. A. Peters, 2009a). In what senses was this so? Membership, having exceeded 100 within just a few years of PESA's birth, was by 2002 reduced to 24 (Haynes, 2009, p. 740). One by one, branches disappeared. Informal groupings within and between cities and regions continued, but the primary means for bringing members together became the annual conference and that too was experiencing difficulties. In 2000, one senior member even foreshadowed a motion (for the 2001 conference) 'that PESA disbands forthwith', but in the event the motion was never put (p. 740). Attendance at the 2002 conference in Brisbane reached a new low of just 12, despite the introduction of subsidies for student presenters (p. 740). It became increasingly difficult to find enthusiastic offers of assistance with executive duties and conference organisation. Perhaps most significantly, scholars who retired or left to take up positions elsewhere were often not replaced with philosophers of education and in some cases were not replaced at all.

From 2003, PESA has witnessed a sustained revival in its fortunes. The Auckland conference that year was well attended and included substantial contributions from many who had hitherto had little or no involvement with the Society. Indigenous perspectives on educational theory were represented at this event to a greater extent than had ever previously been the case. A good number of doctoral students participated, many for the first time. Matters of policy were engaged energetically and rigorously. Conferences in subsequent years have been similarly successful, each in distinctive ways. The venues have varied from 'conventional' locations such as Melbourne (2004, 2013, 2015), Sydney (2006), Brisbane (2008), and Auckland (2011) to Hong Kong (2005), Hawaii (2009), Taiwan (2012), Fiji (2016), the Te Papa Museum in Wellington (2007), and a farm in Western Australia (2010). Participants now come from a far wider range of countries than in the past, with delegates in recent years from Asia, Africa, Europe and North America as well as Australia and New Zealand. The themes and questions addressed in conference papers have also broadened considerably. Membership levels are now comparable with those attained at the high water mark in the 1970s. The Society's journal, *Educational Philosophy and Theory*, is thriving. It is widely regarded, with *Educational Theory*, the *Journal of Philosophy of Education*, and *Studies in Philosophy and Education*, as one of the top periodicals in the field. Under the editorship of Michael Peters for more than two decades now, the journal has substantially increased its international readership, its submission rate, and the number of issues published each year. The shift to a commercial publisher has added significantly to the Society's finances and allowed new initiatives such as doctoral scholarships to be funded. Each year the journal includes a number of special issues, some of which are subsequently published as stand-alone monographs.

Yet, during this period of recovery, there is much that has remained problematic. New positions in philosophy of education, advertised in those terms, have become exceedingly rare. Several active members of the Society have been appointed to chairs in New Zealand universities (e.g., Peter Roberts at the University of Canterbury in 2008, Michael Peters and Tina Besley at the University of Waikato in 2011, and Jayne White and Carl Mika at the University of Canterbury in 2021), but those positions were not advertised specifically in philosophy of education. Others have been promoted to full professorial status within their institutions (e.g., Robin Small at the University of Auckland, John Ozolins at Australian Catholic University, and Nesta Devine and Andrew Gibbons at Auckland University of Technology). For appointments at Lecturer and Senior Lecturer level, philosophers of education have seldom been targeted. This does not mean no philosophers of education have been appointed in recent years. In New Zealand and Australia, as in Britain and a number of other parts of the Western world, those who regard themselves, 'at heart', as philosophers of education often have to find their way into university positions via other means. They gain, or already hold, appointments in other areas such as curriculum studies, pedagogy, higher education, early childhood education, literacy and language education, or educational policy. Some are based in departments outside Education and others are not in university positions at all. The annual conference provides an opportunity for scholars occupying these widely varying roles to, as it were, come out of their burrows and meet up with kindred intellectual spirits again for a few days, before returning to their respective institutions and organisations.

Somewhat ironically, while there appears to be little enthusiasm among many in positions of power within faculties and colleges of Education to maintain or enhance philosophy of education as an area of study, interest from prospective doctoral students, at least in some locations, is greater than ever. At the University of Canterbury, for example, demand for supervision of philosophical PhD theses in Education has, at times, been so high that students have had to be turned away. With relatively few specialist philosophers of education left in New Zealand universities, and with those who remain often heavily committed with undergraduate and Masters teaching and service responsibilities, there is a limit to how many doctoral thesis students can be taken on at any one time. Even so, there have been cases of New Zealand philosophers of education carrying ten or more senior supervisions at doctoral level. The growing involvement of doctoral students in the life of the Society is also a notable feature of the conferences over the last decade or more, and this has been not just via the presentation of papers but also through contributions to administrative work, the reviewing of papers, and the organisation of special events. As has been suggested elsewhere (Roberts, 2009), this is, to a considerable extent, where hope for the future lies. PESA will depend on these newer and younger scholars for its sustenance, growth and vitality in the years ahead. This is true of sister organisations such as PESGB and PES as well. With a substantial proportion of the academic staff in New Zealand faculties and colleges of education aged over 50, the need to keep injecting 'fresh blood' into the field, while also respecting the wisdom that experience and advancing years can bring, becomes all the more obvious.

Simply asserting this, however, does not make it so, and the impediments to further growth in the field should not be underestimated. Both PESA as a research organisation and philosophy of education more generally need to be examined in the light of broader social, economic and educational changes. The neoliberal turn in policy reform agendas across many countries of the Western world over the last four decades has, as previous chapters have argued, had far reaching consequences for higher education and has marked philosophy of education deeply. There is no *one* neoliberalism but among the different variants several features are common. Neoliberals place great faith in 'the market' as the playing field on which economic and social activity should operate. They value competition between 'providers' and choice for 'consumers'. They regard education and knowledge as commodities to be sold and purchased. Education is seen not as a public good but as a private benefit. State involvement in individual lives should, in theory, be minimised. Institutions are expected to emphasise performance and efficiency, and to work aggressively in creating their distinctive 'brand' in the international higher education marketplace.

These core ideas began to take hold in Britain from 1979 (with the election of Margaret Thatcher as Prime Minister), in the United States from 1980 (with Ronald Reagan taking up the role of President), and in New Zealand from 1984 (with the election of the fourth Labour government). Through the 1980s and 1990s neoliberal ideas also exerted a dominant influence in Australia, Canada, and many other countries. With the adoption of 'Third Way' policies under New Labour in the United Kingdom, new progressivism in the United States under President Clinton, and their offshoots in other parts of the world, we have witnessed the emergence of new discourses on the role of education in building of knowledge economies and societies, but many of the fundamental tenets of neoliberalism remain. The economic crises that have unfolded across North America and Europe from 2008 have, for the most part, been seen by governments not as a signal to invest further in higher education but as a justification for cuts in spending. The Covid-19 global pandemic in 2020 and 2021 has strained university budgets even further, with redundancies and enticements for early retirement rolled out in some parts of the world. Crises of these kinds have been seen not as an opportunity to undertake a fundamental revaluation of the assumptions at the heart of neoliberal global capitalism; rather, the push has been to return to 'business as usual' as soon as possible.

How has philosophy of education fared under these influences? In some respects, it has suffered greatly. Neoliberalism, whatever form it takes, is strongly instrumentalist in orientation. Philosophy of education is, accordingly, seen by many as 'useless' – as a waste of time given its lack of exchange value in the market (within and beyond the educational sphere). In a world where what counts is that which can be measured (see Biesta, 2010; Roberts, 2021a) and, in one way or another, *sold*, philosophy of education is often regarded as of limited value. In teacher education programmes, in-depth philosophical work has largely disappeared (Clark, 2011). The emphasis, in both initial teacher education (e.g., BEd degrees) and graduate or post-graduate diploma programmes, is more on curriculum content courses and the practicalities of classroom life. Philosophy of education is not alone in its marginalisation here, with other traditional disciplinary areas such as sociology and history also having been pushed aside in favour of supposedly more 'relevant' courses. Liberal arts programmes in Education have struggled to survive as neoliberalism has strengthened its grip over higher education institutions, and it is now rare indeed to find specialist courses in philosophy of education available at each level of study. Students are thus often ill-prepared for the demands of Masters or doctoral study in an area to which they have sometimes had only patchy exposure as undergraduates. Even if the will is there to allow further courses in philosophy of education – and usually it is not – there will seldom be sufficient staffing to cover this. While there have been periods of considerable expansion in the total number of academics within faculties and colleges of Education over the last three decades (as well as periods of retraction), philosophy of education has for the majority of that time been seen as increasingly unnecessary. At best, it seems, it can be tolerated provided there are just one or two token specialists in the area; or, it is assumed that anyone can teach philosophy of education and that 'philosophical content' can be added as necessary to other courses.

PESA's history has been shaped significantly by these wider trends but there is no simple correspondence between its fortunes and the rise of neoliberalism. The resurgence in membership and conference participation since 2003 has come at a time when specialist appointments to philosophy of education positions have declined, when the commodification of knowledge has been pushed further than ever before, and when cultures of performativity have become solidly entrenched in universities and other institutions. In one sense, neoliberal policy reform has helped sustain PESA: it has provided on-going fodder for critical analysis. Among New Zealand academics, philosophers of education have been to the fore in not only engaging policy but also identifying and deconstructing its often confused and confusing mix of ideas from different trends and traditions (Roberts, 2019a). At a time when instrumentalist thinking has been very much in the ascendency, PESA, on the face of it an organisation out of step with our age, has gained renewed strength. This can in part be explained by the success of *Educational Philosophy and Theory* and the income generated by this; credit must also go to those who have worked hard in upholding Executive duties within the Society during this period. But there is arguably something deeper at work here, and this requires a certain rethinking of the role of philosophy of education in the contemporary world. It also demands of us that we take a closer, more critical examination, of ourselves. In the next section, I develop these points via the work of the renowned historian of ancient philosophy, Pierre Hadot.

'IT WAS THE BEST OF TIMES, IT WAS THE WORST OF TIMES ...'   81

3   Philosophy of Education as a Way of Life

Hadot (1995) argues that philosophy in the Hellenistic and Roman eras was fundamentally a *way of life*. While each of the different schools of thought – Platonism, Aristotelianism, Epicureanism, Stoicism, Scepticism, and so on – had its own distinctive focus, all were united by a concern to make philosophy more than a discourse *about* philosophy. The Stoics, for example, when teaching philosophy, divided it into theories of physics, ethics and logic; when it came to philosophy as *lived*, however, these different elements came together to form a unity. Philosophy for the ancients was 'a mode of existing-in-the-world, which had to be practiced at each instant, and the goal of which was to transform the whole of the individual's life' (p. 265). Philosophical theories, at Hadot puts it, were in the service of the philosophical life. For some, such as Socrates, Aristotle, Epicurus, the Cynics, and the Stoics, philosophy was the means through which one attained independence and inner freedom (*autarkeia*) – a state in which the ego depended only on itself (p. 266). At stake here was the question of how the human self might free itself from everything alien to it. For the Epicureans and the Stoics, another dimension was added: the notion of cosmic consciousness. This was the idea that we are part of the cosmos, and that at every moment we should be conscious of living in that cosmos, in harmony with it. Cosmic consciousness permits a 'dilation of our self throughout the infinity of universal nature' (p. 266). Philosophical activity was directed toward *wisdom*. Those who achieved this, the ancients believed, would experience peace of mind (*ataraxia*), but working toward this state would require 'a radical conversion and transformation of the individual's way of being' (p. 265).

For Hadot, a philosophical life is not merely the application of theory to everyday problems. 'The act of living in a genuinely philosophical way', Hadot says, '... corresponds to an order of reality totally different from that of philosophical discourse' (p. 268). For the Stoics and the Epicureans in particular, 'philosophizing was a continuous act, permanent and identical with life itself, which had to be renewed at each instant' (p. 268). The key in both schools of thought was *attention*. For the Stoics, this meant bringing our individual will into line with reason and the will of universal nature; for the Epicureans, the focus was on the pleasure of existing. 'Pleasure' here does not mean merely satisfying one's wants. Rather, in paying attention to our existence, we must engage in a constant process of working on ourselves. This can involve meditative exercises of various kinds, reflection on one's conscience, and sharpening one's awareness of the finitude of life. (Plato held that philosophy is a training for death: p. 269.) A quite specific orientation to time, and our existence in it, is required:

> Both the Stoics and the Epicureans advised us to live in the present, letting ourselves be neither troubled by the past, nor worried by the uncertainty of the future. For both these schools of thought, the present sufficed for happiness, because it was the only reality which belongs to us and depends on us. Stoics and Epicureans agreed in recognising the infinite value of each instant: for them, wisdom is just as perfect and complete in one instant as it is throughout an eternity. (p. 268)

Hadot maintains that philosophy conceived in this manner is 'not linked to political circumstances, or to a need for escape mechanisms and inner liberty, in order to compensate for lost political freedom' (p. 269). For the ancients, commitment to philosophy as a way of life remained constant across a range of different forms of political organisation and periods of great turmoil and upheaval. It was in the Middle Ages that a major shift occurred, and we are living with the legacy of this to the present day. In the Middle Ages, and with the emergence of the first universities, philosophy became 'a purely theoretical and abstract activity' (p. 270). Theology and philosophy became bound together, and were taught in the service of the medieval church. Universities became institutions for training professionals: 'Education was thus no longer directed toward people who were to be educated with a view to becoming fully developed human beings, but to specialists, in order that they might learn how to train other specialists' (p. 270). This Scholasticism is still evident in philosophy today: philosophy is now predominantly seen as a subject set out in books and taught by professors in university classrooms (pp. 270–271). Hadot concedes that, if we look across the centuries from the medieval period to the 20th century, exceptions can be identified. He mentions Spinoza, Schopenhauer, Nietzsche, and Heidegger, among others, as examples. But the fact remains that philosophy in its modern form 'appears above all as the construction of a technical jargon reserved for specialists' (p. 272).

From the ancients, Hadot argues, we can learn the importance of living, with attention, in the present; of experiencing 'the infinite value of each present moment' (p. 273). The philosopher who lives in this way has a sense of belonging to a whole, a cosmos, that goes behind the limits of his or her individuality. Such an approach can never be reduced to an exact science. Scientific knowledge concentrates on that which is objective and mathematical; cosmic consciousness focuses on the lived experience of the unique, perceiving Subject. To live philosophically in this way is not to escape from the world; nor is this a

'IT WAS THE BEST OF TIMES, IT WAS THE WORST OF TIMES ...'

form of purely self-centred individualism. Philosophy in antiquity 'required a common effort, community of research, mutual assistance, and spiritual support' (p. 274). Philosophers saw themselves as servants to their fellow citizens; they wanted to have an effect on their cities and transform society. Acting not just as one wished but in accordance with justice was a pivotal element in a well-lived philosophical life. Wisdom consists in the ability to maintain a state of equilibrium, where inner peace is combined with – indeed, in part created by – passionate but reasoned action in the face of injustice and human misery (p. 274).

What can we adopt from Hadot's account that might be helpful in understanding the present state of philosophy of education – and in contemplating its possible futures? In many ways, the field conforms to the 'Scholastic' approach to philosophy described by Hadot. The very notion of referring to philosophy of education as a field of study serves to reinforce this point. We have journals devoted to philosophy of education; we write and read books on the subject; we teach it and learn it. We use languages that are often specialised – words, ideas, forms of expression – and do so in the company of others who share, to a greater or lesser extent, those same languages. We play a role, albeit a declining one, in preparing people for professions. We work in institutions with rules, procedures, and structures that set limits, and often quite restrictive ones, on the forms of philosophical activity in which we can engage. We publish and present, knowing we will be evaluated, compared with others and ranked. We have automated systems for submitting and reviewing our work. This all seems a long way removed from 'philosophy as a way of life', as practised in antiquity, with its attention to wisdom, inner peace and cosmic consciousness. But let us ponder our contemporary situation a little more carefully before passing judgement on ourselves.

Part of the problem here is that little term 'we', used persistently in the paragraph above. Who are 'we' in this context? 'We' are the scholars who collectively make up the international philosophy of education community. But this statement simply invites further questions: What *is* 'the international philosophy of education community'? Is it just those who participate in conferences and publish in the journals? Which conferences, and which journals? Who else might be included? And even if we concentrate on conferences and journals that explicitly promote themselves under the banner 'philosophy of education', what might we say about the 'we' represented therein? I cannot hope to provide comprehensive answers to these questions in the space available; nor shall I even attempt to address them all. Rather, I have raised them in order to highlight a key feature, as I see it, of the contemporary philosophy of education world: our relative heterogeneity, diversity and complexity. Note that the qualifier 'relative' has been used here, for three reasons. First, philosophy of education is perhaps less heterogeneous and diverse than it could or should be. Marjorie O'Loughlin (2009) observes that PESA was slow to embrace feminist currents of thought, and a number of scholars have highlighted the need for greater recognition of indigenous knowledge in philosophical discussions of education (Clark, 2006; Mika, 2015; Mika & Stewart, 2016; Stewart, 2018; Stewart & Roberts, 2016). Other silences and gaps could no doubt be identified elsewhere. Second, while the field now includes what some (e.g., Wilson, 2003) see as a bewildering and problematic array of different perspectives, interests and topics, this is not intended to imply that it was somehow lacking in complexity in earlier years. Within PESA, there have always been sharp differences between scholars, sometimes expressed in tense exchanges at conferences, but each decade has brought its own new questions and problems to be addressed. Third, while there is much that makes us different from each other in the current world of educational philosophy, there is also much that we have in common.

John Wilson (2003) argues that 'there is no well-established tradition in philosophy of education, either as regards its methodology or as regards its subject-matter, as there is in other branches of philosophy' (p. 279). He claims that '[w]hen we speak of the psychology or sociology of education, of someone studying as an historian or an economist, we seem to know pretty well what we are talking about' and that '[a] contemporary historian of education ... can be recognised as doing much the same sort of thinking in much the same sort of way as an historian of education a hundred years ago' (p. 279). He laments the fact that 'there appears to be no single perspective on the philosophy of education', and suggests that now '[m]ore or less anything goes', citing a selection of titles from the PESGB proceedings of 2001 as evidence for this (p. 280). 'The contributions', he says, 'are bewildering ("Foucauldian influences in the turn to narrative therapy", "The promise of Bildung", "Waiting on the Web", "Reconsideration of Rorty's view of the liberal ironist as the post-modern ideal of the educated", and so on): not only do the topics vary, but there is no single style or genre of discourse' (p. 280). Given this situation, it will, he maintains, be necessary to 'start more or less from scratch' (p. 281) in rethinking and rebuilding the field.

I find almost every point noted above problematic. As others have already offered detailed critiques of Wilson's paper (Hogan, 2006; Standish, 2006), let me make just a few remarks that are relevant to the present discussion. There *are* well established tradition*s* (the plural is important here) of philosophical inquiry in education, with well-trodden but constantly evolving key concerns as far as subject matter is concerned and considerable agreement on some key aspects of methodology (cf. Vokey, 2006). Psychology, history and sociology are no less complicated than philosophy of education, and to suggest that an historian of education today will be little different in the way he or she approaches the subject from his or her counterpart of a century ago beggars belief. Why would we expect a 'single perspective' on philosophy of education? I cannot think of a single field of study taught over several decades at university level where this would be the case. It is not clear to me what Wilson finds so objectionable or bewildering in the titles he lists as examples, and it seems hardly surprising that there should be more than one style of writing and discourse at an international academic conference. Philosophy of education need not be seen as a 'branch of philosophy' at all. (I am aware that this view is at odds with the position taken in some collections on philosophy of education: e.g., Siegel, 2009.) Finally, it is, I would argue, *impossible* to 'start from scratch'; we must work with what we have, with circumstances as we find them, living and participating as scholarly beings shaped but never completely determined by the history that has gone before us.

Wilson is not a lone figure here. Elsewhere, concerns have been expressed about philosophers of education addressing 'trivial' matters, 'unrelated to major educational problems' (Vandenberg, 2009, p. 786). Needless to say, there are differing views on what counts as trivial and what really matters, and where such judgements need to be made, due attention must be paid to questions of purpose and context. Another way to look at these commentaries, however, is to see them as a sign of a field of study in good health. Philosophers of education demonstrate, through their actions, what philosophy of education involves and one principle most hold dear is the importance of questioning and debate. More than this, however, work that raises important questions about the current state of philosophy of education allows us to step back for a moment and pause to reflect on the 'bigger picture'. Why do we see ourselves as philosophers of education at all? What gives a commitment to philosophy of education substance and meaning? Why does our field matter in today's world? Philosophy of education is neither a single tradition with one methodology and complete agreement on key problems and questions *nor* an 'anything goes' affair. Most philosophers of education, I would wager, are concerned in some way with questions of meaning and value, judgement and consequences, in the pedagogical realm. What they disagree on, of course, is precisely how such questions should be formulated and how they should be answered. An analytic philosopher of education may differ from a Marxist in the methods of inquiry adopted but the standards of good scholarship for both are likely to include clarity in the delineation and discussion of key concepts, soundness in argumentation, sharpness in critique, and coherence and cohesion in the position advanced.

So, where does this leave us as far as 'philosophy of education as a way of life' is concerned? And what are the prospects for philosophy of education in the future? The unfriendly soil on which philosophy of education as a subject falls in a neoliberal world, if anything, gives Hadot's argument renewed relevance. It is important to be as honest as we can in assessing the realities of the present. We should keep fighting to bring back robust programmes in philosophy of education – from early undergraduate study to doctoral level. We should seek to show how and why philosophy of education is important for teachers (cf. Arcilla, 2002; Carr, 2004; Clark, 2011), and keep doing so as new reviews of teacher education programmes arrive every few years. We should argue strongly for new appointments in philosophy of education. But if current trends continue, we are likely to lose many of these struggles, and long term survival will often depend on choosing one's battles carefully. There is a need to also be thoughtful, creative and 'strategic' (if I might use that now tainted word) in endeavouring to create spaces for rigorous philosophical work in education, despite the formidable institutional, political and ideological barriers to this. This may mean forming alliances with scholars in other areas, taking on leadership roles in key programme areas, and keeping an open mind about what counts as philosophy of education. Sometimes we will need to rename what we do. 'Educational theory', for example, can include philosophy of education but also encompass theoretical sociology of education, cultural studies, and gender studies, among other areas. The boundaries between these fields are neither fixed nor rigid (see further, Roberts, 2018).

Bringing Hadot's ideal to life in current contexts is by no means easy but this is precisely why it matters now more than ever. To make philosophy of *education* a way of life is to commit to process of lifelong learning, irrespective of whether one is or is not employed in an institutional position. As the earlier brief history of PESA indicated, this is one area where a significant shift has taken place. In the 1970s, a majority of PESA conference participants were appointed specifically to teach philosophy of education in universities; now such people are in the minority. Philosophy of education as a way of life need not be confined to those 'named' as philosophers of education. A philosophical life in education is one devoted to rigorous inquiry, to the in-depth investigation and exploration of *ideas*, in a community with others so inclined, and this can occur not merely in conferences or university classrooms but in schools and early childhood centres, in informal adult learning groups, in union activities, in libraries and café discussion groups. Some may worry that this represents a diluting of the field, a retreat from the discipline that governed philosophy of education as it was taught in the 1960s and 1970s. My response to such concerns would be to say 'not so', at least not when viewed in relation to a larger set of goals. Those who do remain in university posts can themselves circulate well beyond their institutions and become involved in teaching and learning, of a less formal and easily measured kind, elsewhere. They are likely to become better university teachers for that broader contact. Equally, there is value in opening up university teaching to include contributions from members of the wider community, and in some parts of the world this is routine practice.

4   Conclusion

If we wait for perfect conditions to usher in a rosy future for philosophy of education, we will wait forever. As Hadot's ancients counselled, we must make the most of the present, living every moment to the fullest, aware that we are just one part of a much larger picture. Philosophy of education currently has much to celebrate: vibrant Societies of diverse scholars committed to the field, strong interest in doctoral study, thriving journals, and fresh, rigorous, insightful thinking in addressing questions of importance. Simultaneously, these are also, in other important ways, the worst of times. The grim employment situation of recent years is unlikely to be overturned any time soon, if at all. Teachers are entering their profession not knowing who we are talking about when we mention John Dewey, R.S. Peters, Jane Roland Martin, Nel Noddings, Plato, or Rousseau. But what is worst in the current environment – the dehumanising narrowness of neoliberal, technocratic thinking in education – can also become the territory on which something worthwhile is built. For, just as our predecessors in antiquity had to remain focused on their goals in the midst of political turmoil, so too must we not lose sight of ours. Staying attentive and quietly committed in the eye of storm, so to speak, by engaging current policy and institutional trends critically, calmly and systematically, builds the kind of strength and perspective that will serve us well as philosophers of education in the years ahead.

Acknowledgement

This chapter is a revised version of Roberts, P. (2013). 'It was the best of times, it was the worst of times ...': Philosophy of education in the contemporary world. *Studies in Philosophy and Education*, *34*(6), 623–634. With kind permission from Springer Science+Business Media.

CHAPTER 6

A Philosophy of Hope

Pedagogy, Politics and Humanisation

1 Introduction

Of all the different domains of educational study, few are more diverse, complex and contested than critical pedagogy. Critical pedagogy is a multidisciplinary field of inquiry, informed and shaped by a wide range of intellectual traditions and theoretical perspectives. Critical pedagogues can, for example, be humanists, existentialists, Marxists, socialists, feminists, postmodernists, or post-colonialists, or various combinations thereof. There is no universally accepted 'definition' of critical pedagogy; nor is there an agreed account of exactly how the field has progressed and developed. There are, nonetheless, some key ideas at the heart of work in this domain. Critical pedagogues, for all their differences, share a commitment to social justice, democratic struggle, and the value of questioning and critique. They seek to allow the voices of those who have been marginalised to be heard. They stand opposed to authoritarianism and to discrimination in all its forms. Critical pedagogy is concerned with identifying, analysing and transforming oppressive structures, practices and relations, even if there may be considerable debate over how oppression and transformation are best understood. Critical pedagogues are also united in the view that education is a political process, underpinned by an implied or explicit set of assumptions, values and ideals. Many who work in the field point to both limits and possibilities in the role of education as a force of social change. Education, it is argued, can play a part in reinforcing existing inequalities, but it can also be crucial in contesting and addressing those inequalities.

Before turning to the main focus of this chapter, a brief comment on the constituent elements of the term 'critical pedagogy' is in order. The 'critical' element of critical pedagogy does not refer to the mere act of *criticising* (though that can be part of it) or to *criticism* of the literary kind (though literature too might be addressed by some critical pedagogues). Critical pedagogy, in its many different forms, is also usually distinguished from 'critical thinking' as espoused by some analytic philosophers. Critical pedagogy implies a willingness to examine and engage not just texts, ideas or arguments but also hierarchies of power and privilege in economic, political and cultural systems and institutions (Apple, 1999; Darder, Torres & Baltodano, 2017; Kincheloe, 2007,

© BLOOMSBURY PUBLISHING, 2021 | DOI:10.1163/9789004518179_007

A PHILOSOPHY OF HOPE

2008a; McLaren, 1989; Steinberg, 2007). Critical engagement with contemporary developments in policy – e.g., under globalisation and neoliberalism – is also common (Giroux, 2006, 2008; Kumar, 2016; Leistyna, 2007; Nikolakaki, 2012). Critical pedagogy focuses not just on theorising and discussing but also on resistance, and, in some cases, on revolution (Giroux, 1983; McLaren, 2000). The 'pedagogy' aspect of critical pedagogy is likewise at odds with some common interpretations of this term. Pedagogy for critical pedagogues is not simply 'teaching methods'. Indeed, scholars working in this field are often sharply critical of the obsession with methods in teaching (Aronowitz, 2012; Benade, 2012; Macedo, 1997). Methods need to be appropriate to *contexts* (Kincheloe, 2008a; Roberts, 2000). Thus, for critical pedagogues, knowing *how* to teach also involves knowing *why* one is teaching. Knowledge is a contested domain, with not merely the question of truth but also matters of justice at stake (cf. Kincheloe, 2008b). A critical pedagogue always needs to ask: What do I stand for, and why? With whom am I working? Under what circumstances? Seen in this light, pedagogy can be conceived as the theory and practice of teaching, as enacted in specific situations, with particular groups, pursuing given ends, with both constraints and opportunities for worthwhile educational change.

Critical pedagogy's eclectic nature is reflected in both its philosophical heritage and its links with other domains of study. With its emphasis on change and transformation, it builds on the tradition of progressive education established by John Dewey, W.E.B. DuBois, Carter G. Woodson, Myles Horton, Herbert Kohl, Jonathan Kozol, Maxine Greene, Samuel Bowles and Herbert Gintis, Martin Carnoy, and others, and on the writings of radical critics of institutional life such as Ivan Illich (Darder, Baltodano & Torres, 2017, pp. 3–5). Antonio Gramsci's ideas on hegemony and organic intellectuals, and the Critical Theory of the Frankfurt School, as represented by thinkers such as Max Horkheimer, Theodore Adorno, Herbert Marcuse, and Jürgen Habermas, have also exerted a formative influence (Giroux, 1983, 1988; Kellner, Lewis, Pierce & Cho, 2009; Kincheloe, 2008a; Mayo, 1999; Morrow & Torres, 2002; Peters, Lankshear & Olssen, 2003). Among more contemporary scholars, Joe Kincheloe, himself a leader in the field, names the following as key figures: Stanley Aronowitz, Henry Giroux, Michael Apple, bell hooks, Donaldo Macedo, Peter McLaren, Ira Shor, Jesus 'Pato' Gomez, Ramon Flecha, Deborah Britzman, Philip Wexler, Patti Lather, Antonia Darder, John Willinsky, Shirley Steinberg, and Ana Cruz (Kincheloe, 2008a, pp. 75–103). There are also close connections between critical pedagogy and other related bodies of work such as those devoted to critical literacy (Lankshear & McLaren, 1993; Wallowitz, 2008), critical media studies (Hammer & Kellner, 2009; Kellner, 1995, 2003), aesthetics and arts education (Lewis, 2012), ecopedagogy (Kahn, 2010), and critical whiteness studies (Rodriguez & Villaverde, 2000).

There is one notable omission from the key thinkers mentioned thus far: Paulo Freire, arguably the most important figure of all in the development of critical pedagogy as a field of study. Born in 1921 in Recife, Brazil, Freire first gained international acclaim in the early 1970s with the publication of his classic text, *Pedagogy of the Oppressed* (Freire, 1972a). The developer of a highly successful, critical approach to adult literacy, Freire was exiled from his home country when the military seized power in 1964, taking up residence in Chile and later Switzerland, where he continued to refine and extend his educational ideas. In high demand as a speaker and consultant for educational programs the world over, Freire was able to return permanently to Brazil in 1980. Having established his name with his early books, *Education: The Practice of Freedom* (Freire, 1976), *Pedagogy of the Oppressed* (Freire, 1972a) and *Cultural Action for Freedom* (Freire, 1972b), Freire was relatively 'quiet' as a writer from the mid-1970s to the mid-1980s, before gaining a strong scholarly second wind from 1987 onwards. In the last decade of his life, he authored many books on pedagogy, literacy and politics, several of which were composed via dialogues with others (Escobar et al., 1994; Freire & Faundez, 1989; Freire & Macedo, 1987; Freire & Shor, 1987; Horton & Freire, 1990), others of which reflected on his service as Secretary for Education in the municipality of Sao Paulo (Freire, 1993), his previous publications (Freire, 1994), and his early educational experiences (Freire, 1996). In his later books he paid particular attention to the work of teachers (Freire, 1998a) and to the ethical, political and educational challenges posed by neoliberalism (Freire, 1997, 1998b, 1998c, 2004, 2007). He died in 1997.

Freire has been called the 'Father' of critical pedagogy (Kirylo, 2013, pp. 49–52), the 'quintessential teacher and learner' (Wink, 2011, p. 101), and 'the most influential educational philosopher in the development of critical pedagogical thought and practice' (Darder, Torres & Baltodano, 2017, p. 5). Rather than trying to do justice to the entire field of critical pedagogy – a difficult if not impossible task given the space available – this chapter will focus on Freire and two other scholars who have acknowledged their profound debt to him: Ira Shor and bell hooks. Among the many critical pedagogues who draw heavily on Freire in their work, Shor and hooks are particularly noteworthy for their strong focus on teaching. In their publications and in their pedagogical practice, they have extended and applied Freirean ideas in novel ways. Both are both based in the United States, but the problems addressed in their books resonate with concerns expressed by critical educators across the globe. Freire, Shor and hooks have, collectively, produced an extensive body of published work that continues to speak to the dilemmas and struggles faced by teachers, in both formal and informal educational settings, on a daily basis. The first part of this chapter provides an overview of Freire's educational philosophy, while the second concentrates on Shor and hooks. The chapter concludes with brief reflections on the meaning and significance of hope in Freirean theory and on the possibilities for critical pedagogy in the future.

2   Paulo Freire: Philosophy, Pedagogy, Practice

Paulo Freire occupies an important place in the history of philosophy of education, not just in terms of his theoretical contributions but also for his legacy as an educational practitioner. His ideas emerged from his extensive involvement with adult education in Brazil, Chile, and other countries. His understanding of philosophy, in turn, played a significant role in shaping his educational practice. Freire is an eclectic thinker, with an educational philosophy shaped by multiple intellectual traditions, including liberalism, Marxism, Critical Theory, existentialism, phenomenology, radical Catholicism, and postmodernism (Mackie, 1980; Mayo, 1999; Morrow & Torres, 2002; Roberts, 2000; Schugurensky, 2012; Webster, 2016). He adopts a dialectical approach to understanding reality, informed by his reading of Hegel and Marx, among others (Freire, 1972a, 1972b, 1985; McLaren, 2000; Torres, 1994). He focuses on the dynamic, ever-changing, interactive relation between the material world and the inner world of subjective experience. He accepts the Hegelian principles of all things being in motion and of contradictions giving rise to change, but he is at one with Marx in wanting to apply these ideas to social phenomena. As conscious beings, we have the capacity to reflect on the world and to respond to the content of our reflection through action. ('World' in Freire's philosophy includes both the realm of nature and socially constructed reality.) At the same time, the world, as it were, 'acts back' on us, shaping patterns of thought. Our ideas, feelings, and attitudes are also influenced by our relationships with others, and by the institutions, workplaces, and social spaces we inhabit. We are conditioned but not determined by what the world brings to us (Freire, 1996, 1997, 1998b). This is not a linear process; rather, there is a constant intersecting and intertwining of inner and external worlds. From a Freirean point of view, reality never 'sits still'; there is always a need for further reflection and action. Humans are unique not only in the extent to which, and ways in which, they can reflect but also in their sense of temporality and historical perspective (Freire, 1976). As humans, we can place the events of today in the broader context of past experience and also imagine how the world might be in the future. We act not just on the basis of instinct but with purpose and deliberation, even if there may be substantial variations in the way this occurs.

Freire's epistemology builds on his conception of the nature of reality. Faced with a world that is constantly changing, it follows for Freire that we can never know completely or finally or absolutely. We come to know through our interaction with others and the world, and this is a necessarily ongoing process. Knowledge for Freire is not something that is 'given' to us; we have to seek to know, throughout our lives. What can seem certain at one moment in time may, through further reflection in the light of subsequent observation, interaction or experience, seem less certain, perhaps even utterly misguided, at another moment in time. Consistent with a recognition of knowledge as fluid, contestable, and subject to change, Freire encourages the development of key epistemological virtues (Freire, 1985, 1996, 1998b, 1998c). In seeking to know, he says, we should adopt an open-minded stance, being ever-ready to listen, to watch, and to learn. Knowers are curious beings; they want to ask questions, to investigate, to explore (Freire & Faundez, 1989). Knowing demands rigour and care. Seeking to know is an intellectual process, but it is also more than this. Freire speaks of knowing with his whole body. Knowing is both passionate and rigorous, both disciplined and creative (Roberts, 2005). Knowers are restless beings, always with more work to do. While Freire cautions against being too certain of our certainties, this does not mean that we cannot draw meaningful distinctions between different ways of understanding the world. Freire is not a relativist, in either epistemological or ethical terms; he would have been quite happy to say that some ideas, some ways of interacting with others, some ways of living in the world, are better than others.

At the heart of Freire's ethic is the notion of humanisation (Freire, 1972a). Humanisation means becoming more fully human: more completely what we already are, and were meant to be, as human beings. Freire calls this an ontological vocation. Humanisation is, however, also an historical vocation, for realising the ideal of becoming more fully human entails acting, with others, in the world, as temporal and reflective beings. We become more fully human through engaging in praxis: critical, dialogical, transformative reflection and action (Freire, 1972a; Mayo, 2004; Roberts, 2000). The concept of praxis has ancient origins, dating back, in the West, at least as far as the ancient Greeks, but Freire's interpretation and application of this term can be distinguished from other accounts by its political and social elements. Freire's particular interest is in reflective action that transforms unjust social conditions (Darder, 2002; Rosaz, 2007; Torres, 2014). For Freire, we engage in praxis not on a solitary basis but in solidarity with others. We do so, moreover, not just as rational actors but as emotional beings. From a Freirean point of view, Descartes' declaration 'I think, therefore I am' needs to be replaced with another maxim: 'We think, and feel, and act, in dialogue with others; therefore we are'. Just as knowledge and knowing are necessarily incomplete for Freire, so too is the process of becoming more fully human. We remain unfinished beings, always in the making, always in a state of formation or becoming (Freire, 1996, 1998b). Freire

A PHILOSOPHY OF HOPE

acknowledges that while humanisation may be the ideal, dehumanisation is a reality. Dehumanisation can be witnessed in the impediments placed in the paths of others seeking to become more fully human. These may be imposed by structures, policies, attitudes, or practices. Dehumanisation may be evident at the largest global scale (e.g., in the experience of widespread poverty, malnutrition and disease, or in the violence of warfare) but it can also be present in the smallest moments of daily life (e.g., in 'throwaway' comments with racist or sexist overtones).

In Freirean theory, liberation and oppression are the concrete manifestations of humanisation and dehumanisation respectively. Freire's acknowledgement that dehumanisation is a reality does not mean that he accepts its existence as inevitable; to the contrary, his work is built upon the idea that oppression, as the lived expression and experience of dehumanisation, can be resisted and addressed. Freire saw oppression as a key epochal theme in the 20th century and liberation as a key task (Freire, 1972a, 1976, 1994). Liberation for Freire includes both the process of struggling against oppression and the development of key human virtues. Foremost among these virtues is love, a concept that is always present, directly or indirectly, in Freire's work (Darder, 2002; Fraser, 1997). Freire did not downplay the significance of romantic love, but in his philosophical, pedagogical and political work, his principal concern is with what can be called 'active' love (Roberts & Saeverot, 2018). Love for Freire is a form of deep care and commitment. Freire speaks of loving those with whom we work, the subjects we study, and the very idea of life itself (Freire, 1994, 1996, 1997; Freire & Shor, 1987; Horton & Freire, 1990). In our relations with others, love springs from a recognition of the Other as a fellow thinking, feeling, willing being – a being who may experience sorrow as well as joy, frustration as well as success. In the act of study, love is evident in the attention paid to what we are reading, in the agony and exhilaration we experience as we try to grasp ideas, and in the persistence we display in constantly seeking to know. Freire also stresses the importance of hope (Freire, 1972a, 1994). This was especially significant in the dire situations with which he was dealing as an adult educator. For Freire, despair does not cancel out hope; it gives it its very reason for being (Chen, 2016; Roberts, 2016). Hope from a Freirean perspective is not blind optimism (Rossato, 2005); it is grounded in a sober analysis of the conditions of the present, and a realistic understanding of what is possible in the future. Other virtues that form part of Freire's account of liberation include trust, faith, and critical thinking. Liberation, as Freire sees it, is never given; it is earned, through struggle. Liberation is not merely an individual matter; it is a social process. And, in keeping with the unfinished nature of being human, liberation is never complete. It is not an endpoint, at which one can declare

'Finally, I am now liberated'; rather, the work of liberation continues throughout life, as fresh challenges arise and new actions are taken.

Freire's educational theory builds on these underlying philosophical ideas. Many educationists are aware of his distinction between 'banking' education and 'problem-posing' education (Freire, 1972a), though some of the points Freire makes in drawing that distinction are often lost when there is a reliance on second-hand accounts of his work. In *Pedagogy of the Oppressed*, Freire argues that education has suffered from a kind of narration sickness, with teachers who are expected to pass on knowledge in a monological fashion to passive students. Content under this approach is 'banked' into the minds of passive students, who receive the teacher's knowledge as a gift. This account has led some to believe that Freire was against 'teacher talk' or even against the very idea of teaching. Some have adopted the label 'facilitator', preferring this over what is assumed to be the more directive term 'teacher'. This reading of Freire has been repeatedly contradicted in Freire's own later writings and in the work of other interpreters of his work (Freire, 1987, 1996, 1998a; Freire & Shor, 1987; Horton & Freire, 1990; Mayo, 1999; Roberts, 2000; Schugurensky, 2012; Tan, 2018a, 2018b). The key feature of banking education is its oppressive nature. This is evident in the suppression of questions and of critical thought in the banking system. Under banking education, students are treated not as thinking, feeling, active beings but as pawns in larger game where power is exercised to maintain existing inequalities and injustices. Teachers talking is not in itself the problem; the problem from a Freirean perspective lies in the denial of the possibility of continuing and extending the conversation started by the teacher in collaboration with the students. Freire's opposition is to authoritarian education, and banking education is an example of this. Being authoritarian is, however, not the same as exercising authority or being an authority in a subject area, both of which are necessary in good teaching as Freire conceives of this (Freire & Shor, 1987). Freire is against an 'anything goes' approach to pedagogy, and makes it plain that he is a teacher and not merely a facilitator (Freire & Macedo, 1995). This stance has to do with his characterisation of teaching as an extraordinarily demanding commitment, with important responsibilities, one of which is the obligation to uphold a sense of structure and direction in an educational setting (Freire, 1998a, 1998b; Freire & Shor, 1987).

Problem-posing education begins from the assumption that humans are active, curious, inquiring beings, who can ask questions and pose problems in relation to themselves and the world they encounter (Freire, 1972a). Sometimes called liberating or authentic education, problem-posing education builds on the knowledge and experience students bring with them to an educational environment. Importantly, for Freire, problem-posing education does

A PHILOSOPHY OF HOPE

not simply affirm the views expressed by students; it fosters critical reflection upon those ideas. Respect for differences among students is vital, but so is the principle of being open to having one's existing understanding of the world challenged. Teachers and students in a problem-posing classroom are both involved in the process of deepening and extending understanding, and of creating knowledge, but this does not mean they are the same as each other. Both teachers and students have obligations to their subject area and to other participants in the educational process, but their roles are not identical. Problem-posing education emphasises the fostering of dialogue as a key pedagogical principle, but this is not aimless chatter. Educational dialogue, for Freire, while keeping open opportunities for the unexpected to happen, should have a definite sense of purpose. Freirean dialogue is rigorous and serious (Freire & Shor, 1987). This does not mean it needs to be entirely lacking in humour, or that it should be dull and pedantic. To the contrary, Freire believes: in a structured, purposeful educational conversation, participants will be both passionate and thoughtful, with varied contributions from personalities of many different types. Some participants, Freire recognises, will be more exuberant than others; some will display a quiet earnestness. But regardless of differences, all participants – including the teacher – share a commitment to the subject matter, to each other, and to the ideal of humanisation. One other point must be stressed in capturing what Freire means by problem-posing education: this is not problem-solving education. Freire prefers the former term for at least two reasons. First, in many of the places where he worked as an educator, the problems faced by students were not of a kind that lent themselves to easy or rapid or straightforward 'solutions'. Second, the act of posing problems – of reflecting, clarifying, asking questions, and investigating, and then of doing so again as new problems arise – is as significant as any answers generated by the investigative process (Roberts, 2000, 2010).

Freire's ideas emerged from, and found expression in, the adult literacy and extension programs with which he was involved in Brazil and Chile (Freire, 1972b, 1976). His approach to adult literacy education was based on the understanding that reading and writing can play a role in reinforcing and resisting the status quo. Freire started with the existential realities of the literacy learners, finding out as much as possible about their hopes and dreams, their work experiences, their living situations, their expectations of themselves and others. He found that many participants had a fatalistic attitude toward the world, attributing their circumstances to 'God's will' or destiny. This mode of understanding, he argued, was no accident: it served the dominant interests of landowners and urban corporate and political elites in Brazil at that time. Beginning with words drawn from the world of the learners – e.g., favela (slum) – Freire and his co-workers encouraged participants, in dialogue with others, to reflect on not only their own situation, but also their relations with others, and their distinctiveness as beings of culture and history. New words were quickly generated, and the adult learners moved from seeing themselves as passive recipients of the teacher's knowledge to active participants in the educational process. In his later work, Freire built on these early observations and experiences, theorising literacy at greater length (Escobar et al., 1994; Freire, 1985, 1996; Freire & Macedo, 1987; Freire & Shor, 1987). He developed a notion of critical literacy that focused on the linking of 'word' with 'world', the importance of both challenging and being challenged by a text, and the need for both breadth and depth in university reading (Roberts, 1996a). He spoke of wrestling with texts while loving them, of the joys of reading, and of the beauty of the written word (Freire, 1996; Freire & Shor, 1987).

In his literacy work, and in his educational theory more generally, Freire became widely known for his espousal of 'conscientisation' (Freire, 1972a, 1972b, 1976, 1985). Often misinterpreted as 'consciousness raising', conscientisation for Freire implied the cultivation of one's conscience and the emergence of a deeper, more critical and rigorous understanding of the society in which one lives (Liu, 2014; Roberts, 2000). Conscientisation forms part of Freire's broader understanding of education as a non-neutral, political process (Freire, 1985, 1987, 1997, 1998c, 2004, 2007). The political nature of education is evident at multiple levels, from the global to the local. International testing regimes such as the PISA process can exercise considerable sway over educational policies at a national level. The priorities determined by politicians have an important bearing on what is taught, how, and to whom in schools and other educational institutions. The politics of education will also be evident in the physical layout of a classroom (this may, for example, inhibit or enable discussion), the assessment system that is adopted and applied, the pedagogical methods that are employed, the reading matter that is recommended, and the attitudes, assumptions and ideals teachers and students bring with them to an educational setting. Freire's point is that no teacher can avoid being 'political'; the key is to be as honest and rigorous as possible in understanding, revealing and negotiating the politics of educational life. For Freire, teaching is a necessarily interventionist activity (Roberts, 1996b, 1999b, 2003a, 2016b). Intervention in this context is not the same as imposition. A Freirean teacher must always respect the right of students to disagree, and must seek to listen carefully to what all have to say, avoiding the temptation to thrust his or her own views on others (cf. Escobar et al., 1994; Nieto Ángel, Maciel Vahl & Farrell, 2020; Roberts, 2019b). Teaching can be tremendously powerful in transforming human lives, but it always carries risks and uncertainties (Freire, 1998a, 1998b; Freire & Shor,

A PHILOSOPHY OF HOPE 97

1987). Knowing how to work constructively with those risks, rather than allowing them to become debilitating and obstructive, is one of the hallmarks of liberating education. Freire was highly critical of banking education, but he was a consistent advocate for committed teachers, arguing the need for better salaries and conditions right up to his last writings (Freire, 1998a).

3 Critical, Engaged Teaching: Ira Shor and bell hooks

Ira Shor is one of the most innovative and important interpreters of Freire's work. He and Freire formed a close friendship and co-authored a key text together (Freire & Shor, 1987). Shor has published books on American cultural history (Shor, 1986) and critical literacy (Shor & Pari, 1999), but his principal focus is teaching. His first major work, *Critical Teaching and Everyday Life* (Shor, 1980) has been particularly influential. Subsequent volumes with a pedagogical focus – *Empowering Education* (Shor, 1992) and *When Students Have Power* (Shor, 1996) – have built on the foundation laid by *Critical Teaching and Everyday Life*, with detailed explorations of the pitfalls and rewards that await progressive and democratic teachers. Shor has also played a pivotal role in bringing together other scholars with an interest in Freire's work, editing one of first collections devoted to the practical application of Freirean ideas in classroom settings (Shor, 1987).

Shor, like Freire, emphasises the political nature of education (Shor, 1980, 1992, 1993, 1996). For Shor, politics is not an 'aspect' of teaching or learning; rather, education *is* politics. Politics, Shor argues, 'resides in the discourse of the classroom, in the way teachers and students talk to each other, in the questions and statements from teachers about the themes being studied, in the freedom students feel when questioning the curriculum, in the silences typically surrounding unorthodox questions and issues in traditional classrooms' (Shor, 1993, p. 27). Shor also highlights the politics at work in discriminatory attitudes towards the use of non-standard English in educational institutions, and in the marginalisation of the arts in schools, particularly within poorer neighbourhoods. Inequities in the funding of schools, and the undemocratic administration of them, can also be seen as political matters, worthy of critical interrogation (Shor, 1993, pp. 27–28). Shor proposes a model of critical consciousness that has four qualities: 'power awareness', 'critical literacy', 'desocialization', and 'self-organization' (Shor, 1993, pp. 32–33). His approach focuses on understanding how power is exercised by dominant groups, knowing how regressive patterns of thought (e.g., sexism, racism, classism, homophobia) can become embedded in consciousness, building the analytical habits necessary to provide an in-depth critical reading of the world, and developing an awareness that change is possible.

In the classroom, Shor's critical pedagogy focuses on identifying problems and themes to be addressed dialogically and democratically. He sees participation as a 'door to empowerment' (Shor, 1992, p. 17). In his classes, students are encouraged to place problems that may appear to be local and specific in their broader social, cultural, economic, and historical contexts. Students will often begin with the everyday, with what is most familiar, analysing that in great detail, before moving outwards to establish connections between the object of study and wider structures and practices, both nationally and globally. For American students, the starting point may be something as apparently simple as a hamburger, which, when subjected to critical investigation, reveals itself to be representative of some of the most troubling features of life in their society. A hamburger, when problematised in the manner recommended by Shor, can lead to productive discussion of work, relationships, and even the meaning and purpose of life. Students engage in description, diagnosis and reconstruction (Shor, 1980, p. 157). Classic texts such as Shakespeare's plays need not be seen as lifeless relics from the past; with appropriate prompts and questions from the teacher, they can be brought back to life in the contemporary classroom. *Henry V*, for example, can be linked with questions relating to law, power and war that remain as relevant today as they were in Shakespeare's time (Shor, 1992, pp. 152–155).

Shor notes that, having been nurtured in anti-democratic classrooms, students can at first be reluctant to take up a more active role in the educational process. Mired in testing cultures, students want teachers to provide them with answers. For Shor, pedagogy should be grounded in the issues and controversies that structure the present. Thus, with the culture wars in full swing (Shor, 1986), words like 'liberal' and 'conservative' can form the starting point for critical discussion (Shor, 1992, p. 91). Other themes such as 'utopia' can have application in a variety of educational contexts, at different moments in history (Shor, 1980; see also Roberts & Freeman-Moir, 2013). When power is exercised by students in a democratic classroom, the results will not always be comfortable for teachers, as Shor found out through his own experience (Shor, 1996). Students can, when granted genuine opportunities to determine how and what is taught, and to develop their analytical abilities, turn their critical gaze back on the teacher. Teachers may find themselves having to renegotiate their own roles in relation to practices such as grading, radically disrupting the usual formal institutional expectations. Teachers have to be careful not to promise more than they can deliver, and they must be prepared to live with the 'discomforts of democracy' (Shor, 1996, pp. 82, 150).

A PHILOSOPHY OF HOPE   99

The range of themes and topics addressed by bell hooks, the writing voice
of Gloria Watkins (hooks, 1994a), is impressively diverse. hooks is well-known
for her contributions to scholarship on race and feminism, and for bringing the
experiences and voices of black women to the fore in critical conversations in
these areas (hooks, 1982, 1984, 1989, 1993, 1995). She has been a powerful critic
of racism in American culture and society (hooks, 1992, 1994b, 1995), and has
also addressed questions of class (hooks, 1996, 2000), sex, gender and masculinity (hooks, 1990, 1996, 2004), and place (hooks 2009). Attention here will
be limited to hooks' views on teaching. For hooks, teaching is a transgressive
form of action with the power to subvert and question structures of authority.
Teaching should foster critical thinking of a non-conformist kind. It should,
hooks argues, be unsettling and exciting. Education may sometimes be painful
but teachers should not be afraid to speak of pleasure in the classroom. Teaching entails the acknowledgement of all who are present in a pedagogical situation, and a valuing of the contribution that each participant can make. Radical
pedagogy from hooks' point of view is a collective effort, and the classroom is a
communal space. There is a performative aspect to teaching, though not in the
traditional sense of creating a spectacle nor in the neoliberal sense of enacting
the principle of performativity; rather, the focus is on serving as a catalyst for
engagement. To teach demands a commitment to reciprocity; to the involvement of participants in the performance being enacted. Good teachers seek
to know the students with whom they work, responding to them as unique
human beings. The possibility of mutual recognition must always be present,
even if there may be constraints to the full realisation of such an ideal in given
circumstances. Teaching that 'respects and cares for the souls of our students'
is, for hooks, is a sacred vocation, and in university environments, '[t]he classroom remains the most radical space of possibility in the academy' (hooks,
1994a, pp. 12–13).

Speaking against the 'assembly-line approach to learning', hooks argues for
an engaged pedagogy that emphasises active participation by students in an
environment of mutual recognition (hooks, 1994a, p. 13). She acknowledges
her debt to not just Paulo Freire but also Thich Nhat Hanh, a Buddhist monk
from Vietnam whose work has also been highly influential. hooks embraces
Freire's notion of conscientisation, interpreting this as 'critical awareness and
engagement' (hooks, 1994a, p. 14). She encourages critical thinking as a 'way of
approaching ideas that aims to understand core, underlying truths, not simply
that superficial truth that may be most obviously visible' (hooks, 2010, p. 9).
She admires Freire's open-mindedness and his willingness to accept – indeed,
encourage – constructive critique of his work (hooks, 1994a, pp. 54–56). From
Thich Nhat Hanh's linking of learning with spiritual practice, hooks adopts a

holistic view of education: one where teachers and students regard each other as 'whole' human beings who seek not just the knowledge found in books but also knowledge of how to live in the world (hooks, 1994a, pp. 15–16). From both thinkers, hooks takes the position that reflection must be combined with action. The kind of engaged pedagogy hooks advocates is, she suggests, 'more demanding than conventional critical or feminist pedagogy' (1994a, p. 15). It is a radical approach to education that has a focus on social transformation but also on personal well-being, requiring teachers to attend to themselves as well as the students with whom they work. Teachers, hooks maintains, need to undergo a process of self-actualisation. Thich Nhat Hanh's linking of teaching with healing is important here. The teacher first needs to 'heal' him- or herself in order to be able to best attend to the task of helping others. The academic world tends to stress the role of the intellect, but 'care of the soul' (hooks, 1994a, p. 16) is also needed.

For hooks, traditionally strict boundaries between public and private spheres need to be challenged. Teachers and students in the academy can become unbalanced and 'emotionally unstable' (hooks, 1994a, p. 16). They may want liberating education but resist the idea that the classroom can provide any meaningful therapy in their own lives. hooks, like Freire, insists that students cannot be forced to accept the teacher's views; transgressive pedagogy demands that the freedom of the students be respected and that they take responsibility for their own decisions (hooks, 1994a, p. 19). If students are expected to share and confess in the engaged classroom, the same should be true for teachers. This can be threatening, and learning to be vulnerable can be a challenge for many teachers in higher education. Engaged pedagogy is a risky endeavour, but taking up this challenge opens up new ways of knowing for both students and teachers. Building a sense of community helps in overcoming a preoccupation with safety in the classroom, for then the risks are shared, and all who participate are bound by a 'common good' (hooks, 1994a, p. 40). These pedagogical principles are particularly relevant in classrooms where themes such as racism, sexism and colonialism are addressed. Conflict, hooks argues, need not be a source of despair; instead, there is a sense of solidarity when diversity, dissent and the pursuit of truth are welcomed. Transgressive, engaged pedagogy is not easy; it demands 'struggle and sacrifice', but if this has a sense of purpose and conviction, and if such experiences are shared with others, change is possible (hooks, 1994a, p. 33).

hooks argues that teaching can take place not just in formal institutional environments but also in homes, churches, bookstores, and other settings. Her concept of teaching includes everything from talking with young children to engaging critically with dominant public narratives. In hooks' account,

A PHILOSOPHY OF HOPE

education can take place in the smallest, most intimate moments of engagement between two or more people but is also needed on a much larger scale. hooks calls for 'mass-based political movements' that will foster a commitment to democracy and justice among citizens (hooks, 2003, p. XIII). She acknowledges the genuine progress that has been made by progressive educators, while also drawing attention to the powerful conservative backlash against programs such as women's studies and ethnic studies. In the United States, an ideology of 'imperialist white-supremacist capitalist patriarchy' has been perpetuated, aided by the media, and free speech and dissent have, following the events of 9/11, been undermined (hooks, 2003, p. 11). Those killed in the 9/11 tragedy were an embodiment of 'the world's diversity', but their deaths, instead of providing the impetus to cherish diversity and difference, have prompted rage, intolerance, distortions and simplifications, confusion, and a sense of hopelessness (hooks, 2003, p. 12). Teachers have an important role to play in contesting these trends, but they need to care for themselves if they are to serve others effectively. As hooks sees it, all teachers in professional settings, at any level in the education system, need to take a break from their work at some stage in their careers. Teaching for hooks is a form of service to others, a commitment that is devalued (hooks, 2003, p. 83). Like Freire, hooks sees teaching as an act of love (hooks, 2003, pp. 127–137). Love for hooks fosters greater openness and honesty in teaching and allows teachers to better understand their students. Love does not make teachers less objective; it simply makes them more sensitive and responsive to those with whom they work. Teaching in this way, hooks admits, is very taxing. Given its extraordinary demands, teaching is a vocation that lends itself readily to burnout. Teaching in other, less formal settings, employing a range of pedagogical styles, can provide the sustenance that is necessary for renewal – for regaining the sense of joy that should be a crucial element of education (hooks, 2003, pp. 14, 43).

4   Conclusion: A Philosophy of Hope

In his final years, Freire remained politically and intellectually restless. He was particularly concerned with the encroachment of neoliberal ideas into almost every area of social and economic life (Freire, 1994, 1997, 1998b, 2004, 2007). He spoke scathingly of the ethics of the market, contrasting the attitudes and ideas underpinning neoliberalism with the humanising ideals that had always underpinned his work. Freire saw in neoliberalism a revival of the fatalism that had been dominant among some groups in Brazil during his earlier adult literacy efforts. Neoliberals take it as given that societies should be organised along capitalist lines, and that individuals are motivated by self-interest in their decisions and actions. Freire was open in declaring his support for democratic socialism but he was also always willing to put his views to the test in the company of others. Neoliberals, he felt, were too certain of their certainties; they believed that their way was the only possible way. The dampening down of questions pertaining to the fundamental building blocks of contemporary society and the propensity to denigrate alternatives (or to ignore them altogether) struck Freire as particularly pernicious aspects of the neoliberal consciousness he saw unfolding in the last two decades of the 20th century. Freire stood opposed to neoliberalism on almost every level. Ontologically, the idea of a utility-maximising, competitive individual consumer as the starting point for a discussion of humankind was repugnant to him. Epistemologically, the notion of construing knowledge as a commodity to be bought and sold like other goods in a marketplace was worlds away from his conception of what it meant to know. Ethically and politically, the favouring of 'free' trade, with minimal regulation, by individuals and corporations seeking to maximise their advantage over others, was, for Freire, an affront to the possibility of dialogue, care for others, and collective responsibility for the planet. In educational terms, the prospect of reducing teaching and learning to a system of inputs and outputs designed to enhance efficiency, performance and economic growth was horrific.

The emergence of neoliberalism as the dominant paradigm for economic and social activity was, however, not just a cause for despair; for Freire, it reinforced the need for hope. Neoliberalism, Freire argued, was utterly dehumanising, but it was our response to it that mattered. Freire could see that under neoliberalism, inequalities would widen and our views of what counts as education, knowledge and being human would become steadily narrower. He would have been deeply saddened to see, over recent years, the rise of populist and authoritarian politics in Brazil, the United States, and Europe. In some cases, leaders have been elected on the basis of political rhetoric that is deliberately divisive, anti-intellectual, and often openly sexist and racist. These trends will do much to destroy moves toward greater inclusiveness made by progressive governments in the past, and in education there will be an ever more entrenched focus on narrowly defined, measurable objectives with direct economic value. But it is precisely the desperation created by such policies and practices that gives hope, as an educational virtue, its meaning and significance in our time. Hope is a virtue that cannot be adequately understood purely in abstract terms; it must be lived, and constantly reinvented, as human beings negotiate the changing demands of social, cultural and economic life. If these points are accepted, critical pedagogy becomes more essential than ever. Encouraging students to ask difficult questions about the way they are

A PHILOSOPHY OF HOPE

expected to live in today's world, deliberately setting up opportunities to explore alternative modes of social organisation, and exhibiting qualities that run counter to the spirit of the times (selflessness, humility, openness, and a willingness to listen) can provide hope that change is possible. Hope for Freire, and for Shor and hooks, is neither simply given from one person to another nor generated in a purely individual or internal manner. Instead, it arises from the interaction between two or more people, in dialogue with each other, with a respect for difference that also does not deny what is shared in common. Hope makes most sense not when all is well, when life appears to free and easy, but when situations demand more of us. Thus conceived, hope becomes a profoundly important educational virtue, and a cornerstone of critical pedagogy, providing both the means and the reason for principled, reflective resistance and transformative social change.

Paulo Freire, Ira Shor and bell hooks have all made lasting contributions to the development of critical pedagogy as a field of study. Collectively and individually, they offer something unique and worthwhile to the broader conversations that make up the history of philosophy of education in the West. Their written work is distinguished by a clarity that is sometimes lacking in educational theory; their ideas are conveyed in a manner that is lucid, direct and practical. Across these thinkers, there is an abiding interest in the links and tensions between theory and practice in the pedagogical realm. All three have developed and tested their ideas in the company of the students with whom they have worked. For Freire, Shor and hooks, teaching is a political activity requiring love, care, and commitment. Teachers, they argue, need to have an understanding of what they stand for, of what they value and why. At the same time, they caution, teachers must avoid imposing their truths, their ideals, on students. Teaching should, they suggest, foster a love of learning, respect for others, and a sense of community. Education, they show, is a lifelong process that demands much of all who commit to it. Humanising, engaging, critical education is often uncomfortable, sometimes disruptive and destabilising, and always rigorous.

Critical pedagogy prompts us to examine ourselves and the world in a fresh light. In this sense, it has an inherently 'subversive' character. Those who feel threatened by this will often recoil from the challenges posed by critical scholars and teachers, sometimes responding with anger or defensiveness. But such responses can themselves have educative value, if gently probed and explored. Critical pedagogy may also, in increasingly instrumentalist times, be dismissed as 'irrelevant'. Some may claim that it has no place in contemporary teacher education programmes, suggesting that the focus should be on the more immediate practical demands of the profession. Yet, as the work of Freire, Shor and hooks demonstrates, critical educational theory can be profoundly practical in its orientation, and the activity of teaching is always underpinned by implied theories of what it means to be a human, of the nature of the reality, of what we should favour and why, and of how we should interact and live with others. It could be argued that the biggest 'threat' to critical pedagogy comes, as it were, from within – in the form of theoretical infighting among scholars of differing philosophical and political persuasions. Yet, the history of the field has demonstrated that it has a certain resilience that can withstand – indeed, welcome – critique from both within and without. In the future, it is likely that critical pedagogues will continue to reach out to scholars in other areas, drawing, for example, more heavily on Eastern and indigenous traditions of thought as the field continues to evolve and grow. Critical pedagogy, like all domains of educational study, has its flaws, frictions and fragilities. But its ongoing importance, in some form, seems difficult to deny. Critical pedagogy can enable students to deepen and extend their understanding of social injustices and provide a platform on which to build a narrative of gritty, realistic, grounded hope, whatever the defining economic, social and cultural features of a given epoch may be.

Acknowledgement

This chapter was originally published as Roberts, P. (2021). A philosophy of hope: Paulo Freire and critical pedagogy. In A. Pagès (Ed.), *A history of Western philosophy of education in the contemporary landscape* (pp. 107–128). Bloomsbury. With permission from Bloomsbury Academic, an imprint of Bloomsbury Publishing Plc. (https://www.bloomsbury.com/).

CHAPTER 7

Philosophy of Education as a Way of Life

A Case Study

1 Introduction

My journey into the field of philosophy of education might be described as an accident waiting to happen. As a university student in the early 1980s I enrolled in two Stage One Education papers not with any well-developed professional plan but because the material sounded interesting and the lectures were at times that worked well with my other courses. I initially had no intention of going on to further study in the subject. By the end of that year, I had formed a clear view that I wanted to major in Education. I subsequently completed courses in sociology of education, history of education, comparative education, and other areas of educational study, but philosophy of education was my main focus. A Master's degree, and later a doctorate, followed and now, decades on, I find myself still seeking the forms of understanding philosophy of education can bring. In one sense, then, this is a story of a chance decision taken almost 40 years ago; a story that might very well never have been told. Yet, with the opportunity for self-reflection afforded here, I can see that the 'accidental' path I've taken is one I was always going to take, in some form or another. As a child, I loved to read and to think; I had questions about the meaning of life that demanded answers; and I was troubled by situations, events and interactions that seemed, to my young mind, to be unfair, inconsistent or unhelpful. Philosophy of education has aided me greatly in the process of searching that started early in my life, but this remains very much an incomplete project. In the discussion that follows I set out to show why this is so.

2 Schooling and University Experiences

The oldest of four children, I grew up in Auckland, New Zealand in the 1960s and 1970s. My time at primary school was important in shaping my later educational development. The school I attended for most of my primary years was in a small semi-rural, working class town northwest of central Auckland. Several teachers at the school provided pedagogical models that still influence my educational thinking today. One was quiet and caring, demonstrating the

© KONINKLIJKE BRILL NV, LEIDEN, 2014 | DOI:10.1163/9789004518179_008

distinctive power of gentleness that I would later come to appreciate through reading the *Tao Te Ching* (Lao Tzu, 1963). Another allowed unusual degrees of independence for students, bearing witness to the significance of trust and responsibility in teaching and learning. Such notions, I would discover in due course, were key elements in the pedagogy of Paulo Freire (Freire, 1972, 1998a, 1998b; Freire & Shor, 1987; Horton & Freire, 1990). While not without some periods of difficulty, those years were, overall, the happiest in my schooling life. It was not merely the school teachers I encountered who contributed to my education; equally significant were my family experiences, the friendships I developed, and the myriad activities of boyhood – hut-building, fishing for eels in the river, wandering far and wide, rugby, tennis, athletics, and so on – that collectively, and often silently, taught me how to begin trying to make sense of a complex world. My parents were tireless in their service to the wider community, their own example speaking more insistently to we children about our ethical obligations to others than any words could express. From my friends, with their varied backgrounds, I came to see that solidarity, commitment and companionship could be built across class and ethnic lines, even if I could not have articulated our relationships in exactly that way at the time. During these formative years, I also developed a love of literature that continues to the present day. I recall reading some books from our school library multiple times, swept up in the adventures they described and already seeking out other places, other modes of life, in my child's mind.

I was not a 'bookish' child; equally, I was not one of those boys who regarded reading and study as a waste of time, as something for 'sissies'. Whatever I was doing, whether it was reading, writing, running, riding, talking, or listening, I found it hard to stop thinking, pondering, wondering. I wanted to know: Why are we here? What is our purpose in life? Is there a God? What happens to us after we die? How can we strive to be good? How can we best understand ourselves, others and the world? What should we do when we see or experience injustice? I did not formulate such questions in precisely those terms, but my musings were broadly along these lines. Where some of my friends seemed content to let life 'wash over them', I tended to mull things over at greater length. When I thought I had done something wrong, I would worry about it, sometimes losing sleep over what would now appear to be trivial incidents. I also found myself getting upset when I saw someone else being hurt. The passing of decades can warp recollections of this kind, and there is always a danger of distorting events to make them fit with our current analytical categories. Nevertheless, there are some experiences, some thoughts and feelings, that never leave us, and I can still recall specific events that seemed to show, in a manner comprehensible to a child, just how perplexing and difficult life could be.

If I needed further proof of my vaguely formed convictions about life as a process involving a good deal of searching and struggle, my experience of high school provided it for me. My memories of that period in my educational history are mostly unpleasant, though not without some redeeming features. Almost all my friends from primary school had gone elsewhere for their secondary education, making high school a lonely place, and these were difficult years for other practical and personal reasons as well. There were, however, some sincere and dedicated teachers in different classes, and from them I acquired a keener sense of the seriousness of study and pedagogy. Teaching, I could see, involved a total commitment of one's body, soul and mind. Teaching could be exhilarating but it could also be exhausting. If it wasn't hard to see why so many students found high school alienating, it also wasn't too difficult to appreciate the courage that must have been required by some teachers to continue turning up to their classes, day after day, year after year. While my sense of wellbeing improved at the senior secondary school level, there is much I would rather forget from this period of my life. Of course, that too has been an educational lesson: memories may fade, but one can never fully forget. Part of the despair of education, as I have argued elsewhere (Roberts, 2013a, 2013b, 2016; Roberts & Saeverot, 2018), lies precisely in this: it does not allow us to go back. We cannot return to a state we have left behind but must learn to live with the new forms of understanding education brings, distressing though this may be.

Existentially, high school was troubling, but in academic terms I was fine, and having gained an A Bursary I was ready to begin the next phase of my formal education at the University of Auckland. It was hardly a promising start, with a first year spent on a degree to which I was manifestly ill-suited (a BCom) and mixed success in my examinations. Thereafter I resolved to take the riskier path, switching to a BA degree, with a suite of courses in English, Geography, Anthropology – and Education. The last of these subjects, as noted in the introduction to this chapter, was selected more by chance than design. One of the two Education courses I took was largely devoted to educational psychology; the other was an introduction to Western educational thought. The latter course would prove pivotal in setting me on the path toward a life committed to philosophy of education. The course was taught by Colin Lankshear and Jim Marshall. My tutor was Michael Peters. It was a course of the kind we seldom see these days: a history of educational ideas, beginning with Plato and ending with Freire, having examined Rousseau, Dewey, R.S. Peters, and others along the way. Fascinated by what I discovered in that Stage One Education course, I made a decision to major in Education, and by the end of my second year in the subject was already beginning to ask how I might make this my life's work.

In completing my studies in Education at undergraduate level, I had the good fortune to be taught by a number of excellent scholars from different fields, but philosophical concerns remained to the fore.

Philosophy of education appealed not because it was easy but because it was difficult. Immersion in philosophical work enabled me to challenge some of my hitherto untested assumptions about the social world. I felt uncomfortable yet right at home, as if my life to date – the reading completed, the questions asked, the decisions made, the actions taken, and the relationships formed – had been working towards this moment. I put tremendous effort into my essays for philosophy of education courses, reading, thinking, agonising over what I wanted to say and how I wanted to say it. We learned how to construct and deconstruct an argument, how to unpack educational concepts, and how to compare different theoretical positions. The demands of philosophy of education were exacting but there was, at least in my experience at the University of Auckland, also considerable freedom to explore new ideas. One could be creative but within certain limits, and always with a view to upholding the highest standards of academic rigour.

We were encouraged to read and discuss radical analyses of schooling but also did not ignore liberal and conservative accounts. Works by deschoolers such as Illich (1971) and Marxists such as Harris (1979, 1982) were studied, but due attention was also paid to Peters, Hirst, and others in the analytic tradition of philosophical inquiry (Dearden, Hirst & Peters, 1972; Hirst, 1974; Peters, 1970, 1973). (For an insightful account of the impact of the analytic revolution in philosophy of education, see Waks, 2008.) Postmodern and post-structuralist currents of critical thought were, in Education at any rate, rather less visible at that stage. A more mature reading of Dewey (1966, 1997), Scheffler (1960), and other influential North American figures would also have to wait until later. There were brief forays into original works by Marx (Marx, 1964, 1976; Marx & Engels, 1972), but these too were unfinished journeys. We ventured beyond philosophy of education to consider a number of thinkers who were better known as psychologists (e.g., Fromm, 1942) and sociologists (e.g., Althusser, 1971; Bourdieu & Passeron, 1977; Bowles & Gintis, 1976; Sharp, 1980; Willis, 1977). Among the teachers with whom I studied there was already a strong commitment to social justice in education, and that was to develop further with new appointments in the 1990s.

While this process of intellectual formation was underway, I was simultaneously gaining other forms of life experience, working in a number of different jobs – as a caster in a pottery factory, shoe making, and house hauling, among others – on a part-time or temporary basis. I sometimes regret that I wasn't able to continue with an existence of that kind, engaging in both manual and mental labour for extended periods of time, the different activities complementing

PHILOSOPHY OF EDUCATION AS A WAY OF LIFE

each other. It is easy to romanticise such notions, but there is an important connection, I would argue, between different forms of craftsmanship, where struggle and sweat and tension can co-exist with concentration, skill and careful attention to detail to produce something beautiful – whether this is in the form of a shoe, a piece of pottery, a building, or an academic paper (cf. Roberts & Freeman-Moir, 2013). My experiences on factory floors taught me a good deal about education and the politics of difference; about the links between social class, ethnicity and educational aspirations. Far from resenting the hours I spent pouring liquid clay into plaster moulds, operating leather presses, and preparing houses for removal, I relished the time I devoted to these activities. A less than ideal start to my university studies had turned out to be a blessing in disguise, not only in allowing the 'accident' of finding my way into Education to happen but also in opening up more space for other forms of work, other life experiences outside the academy.

Encouraged by my results in the final year of my undergraduate study, I proceeded directly on to a Master's degree. My courses in the first year of the degree had a sociological and revolutionary flavour as well as an emphasis on the philosophical study of education. One course, unusually for the time (this was the mid-1980s), was entirely devoted to the work of Michel Foucault, with a particular focus on *Discipline and Punish* (Foucault, 1979) and the collection of essays and interviews published under the title *Power/Knowledge* (Foucault, 1980). My Master's thesis addressed Paulo Freire's concept of conscientisation and was supervised by Colin Lankshear, who had inspired me as a teacher from my first contact with him several years earlier. This was the beginning of a research programme of more than three decades. As it turned out, Freire was then on the cusp of his most productive period as a writer, authoring a series of co-authored dialogical books and multiple sole-authored volumes over the last decade of his life (Freire, 1993, 1994, 1996, 1998a, 1998b, 1998c; Freire & Faundez, 1989; Freire & Shor, 1987; Horton & Freire, 1990). There would be no shortage of material for reflection and critical engagement.

I never regarded myself as a 'follower' of Freire, let alone a 'disciple' of him (see Roberts, 2010). Instead, from the beginning I felt that with Freire I was in the company of a fellow traveller – someone with whom I would not always agree but whom I respected for his educational ideas, his strengths as a teacher, and his political and ethical commitment. In my published work, I have argued that Freire must be read holistically, critically and contextually. Given its enormous influence as a text read not just by educationists but by theorists and practitioners in many other fields, *Pedagogy of the Oppressed* (Freire, 1972a) has been the primary focus for many accounts of Freirean ideas. This classic work of critical educational scholarship, by any fair-minded assessment of 20th century educational thought, stands as a landmark in our understanding of the politics of education. It provides a powerful account of oppression and liberation, a rigorous critique of banking education, and a well-developed alternative in problem-posing education. But as Freire himself stressed, there is much more to his corpus of published writings than this one book. When a reading of texts from his earlier and middle writing phases (Freire, 1972a, 1972b, 1976, 1985) is combined with a close examination of the later works cited above, a more rounded, nuanced, complex picture of education and humanisation emerges.

In his later publications, Freire stresses the importance of ethical and epistemological virtues such as humility, openness, curiosity, a willingness to listen, an inquiring and investigative frame of mind, care for the students with whom one works, and political commitment (Peters & Roberts, 2011; Roberts, 2010; Roberts, 2015a, 2022a). He addresses aspects of postmodern thought and acknowledges more fully the multi-layered nature of oppression and liberation. He tackles practical questions relating to the process of teaching, language differences, university reading requirements, and the difficulties of bringing about social change. He talks a great deal about the value of questions, the nature of dialogue and critical thought, the challenges he faced in his adult education work, and the need for gritty, 'armed' pedagogical hope. From these later books, a distinctive approach to critical literacy emerges. The publication of work that had previously enjoyed only limited circulation, via books such as *Pedagogy of Indignation* (Freire, 2004) and *Daring to Dream* (Freire, 2007), has added to ongoing interest in Freire's educational ideas. But Freire welcomed constructive criticism, and at the time of his death in 1997 key areas of his work remained underdeveloped. He was just beginning, for example, to pay more extended attention to the world ecological crisis and its educational significance. There are many other omissions, contradictions and tensions that can be identified (see Roberts, 2000, 2010, 2017a). This is not the place to comment at length on Freire's strengths and weaknesses. The point I want to stress here is that Freire was, in his own terms, an *unfinished* human being: a teacher, husband, father, thinker, and writer who sought to understand himself and the world as deeply as possible, but who realised he could not do this alone and would inevitably fall short in some of his endeavours. In this humble attitude toward his own achievements and struggles, Freire provides a worthy model for other philosophers of education.

3 Academic Life

In 1987, I noticed an advertisement in a daily newspaper for a Junior Lectureship at the University of Waikato, applied as a complete outsider, and after an interview was delighted to be offered the job. The position would begin early the following year. The University of Waikato was located in Hamilton, about two hours' drive south of Auckland, and I will always be grateful to the Education Department there for providing my first step on the academic ladder. The Head of Department was a little embarrassed to discover that I'd spent the night prior to the interview sleeping in my van in a camping ground, having come to Hamilton a day early to prepare. He explained to his new, rather naïve recruit that the Department's budget could have stretched to a room in a motel or hotel. My doctoral thesis was completed on a part-time basis while I was holding down a full-time academic position. I carried a heavy teaching load for several of my first few years at Waikato, making the process of finishing the doctorate doubly difficult, but I was also gaining experience that would serve me well in later years. Among other responsibilities, I taught on large Stage One courses, initially as a tutor, then as a lecturer, and later as both a lecturer and course coordinator. (I was appointed to a permanent Lectureship at the end of my second year in Hamilton.) My time at Waikato not only helped me learn something about the art of teaching; it also provided a good grounding in institutional politics. In addition, it enabled me to expand my research interests to include work on the philosophy of literacy and the higher education curriculum. This would later bear fruit in a series of publications through the 1990s (e.g., Roberts, 1995a, 1995b, 1996a, 1997b, 1997c, 1997d). My contributions in these areas built on my investigation of Freirean themes, which had deepened and extended considerably in completing my doctorate.

At the beginning of 1995, I moved back to a position at the University of Auckland. Our first child had been born a year earlier and our second would arrive just 18 months later. With strong family ties in Auckland (my wife too had grown up there), and with the Education Department experiencing significant growth, this seemed like the right time to make such a move. The department comprised two main academic groups, one of which was Cultural and Policy Studies in Education (CPSE). It would have been difficult, at that time, to find a stronger collection of scholars in critical educational studies anywhere in the southern hemisphere. Within the first year or two of my return to Auckland, my CPSE colleagues had included Roger Dale, Jim Marshall, Michael Peters, Linda Smith, Graham Smith, Alison Jones, Megan Boler, and Susan Robertson, to name but a few. Philosophy of education, sociology of education, educational policy studies, and indigenous education were key strengths of the Education Department at that time. In such an environment, I was able to flourish as a researcher.

While I remained a philosopher of education first and foremost, I also started to write in the policy domain, with work on reforms in qualifications, the curriculum, and tertiary education (e.g., Roberts, 1997a, 1998b, 1999c, 2003b, 2005). I continued to publish on Freire, with my sole authored book, *Education, Literacy, and Humanization* (Roberts, 2000) representing the culmination of much that I had done in the previous decade. I completed the book while on sabbatical leave in 1999, also finishing an edited volume on Freire (Roberts, 1999d) and a co-authored text on university futures (Peters & Roberts, 1999) in the same year. Freire had much to offer, but he was not enough on his own and over the years I have drawn on the work of a number of other thinkers, including Kierkegaard (Roberts, 2013b, 2017b, 2021a), Nietzsche (Roberts, 2001, 2012a), Unamuno (Roberts, 2016; Roberts & Saeverot, 2018), Levinas (Roberts, Gibbons & Heraud, 2015), Lyotard (Roberts, 1998a, 2004), Weil (Roberts, 2011, 2013c, 2021b, 2022b), Beauvoir (Roberts, 2020), and Murdoch (Roberts & Freeman-Moir, 2013; Roberts & Saeverot, 2018). I am not an expert on any of these philosophers, but have simply tried to work with them in productive ways to address key educational questions and concerns.

Kierkegaard is a fascinating figure: an idiosyncratic, deeply committed, highly productive writer, of prime importance in understanding the history of existentialist thought (Carlisle, 2020; Hannay, 2003; Kierkegaard, 1987, 1988, 1989, 1998, 2007, 2009). Unamuno, greatly influenced by Kierkegaard, was similarly enigmatic, passionate in his desire for immortality, despairing of his own critical reason in undermining this. An accomplished novelist as well as philosopher, Unamuno is seldom given the attention he deserves among educationists. I found Nietzsche enjoyable to read, seeing in his work (Nietzsche, 1996, 1974, 1976, 1989, 1996, 1997) and his biography an attempt to make philosophy not merely an academic exercise but a way of life (Hadot, 1995; Solomon, 1999). Levinas has been more difficult. As I have said to one or two friends, reading works such as *Totality and Infinity* (Levinas, 1969) and *Otherwise Than Being or Beyond Essence* (Levinas, 1998) gives me a headache. But sometimes pain of this kind is necessary if we are to make philosophical progress. As an aside, I might note that I found Heidegger's *Being and Time* (Heidegger, 1996) equally challenging, and I have thus far mustered the courage to refer to it only briefly in my work. (I was able to make more headway with 'The Question Concerning Technology': Heidegger, 1997). Simone Weil, a teacher and social activist as well as a remarkable thinker, died at a very young age but left behind a body of work that merits greater recognition from educationists. Like Nietzsche, she was an exemplary exponent of the aphorism as a mode of philosophical expression, and I have revisited some sections of the posthumously published *Gravity and Grace* (Weil, 2001) many times. Lyotard, together with Nietzsche, has enabled me to combine my philosophical and policy interests. His classic work, *The Postmodern Condition* (Lyotard, 1984), as I have argued in earlier chapters of

PHILOSOPHY OF EDUCATION AS A WAY OF LIFE

this book, offers an especially helpful framework for getting to grips with policy changes in New Zealand.

New Zealand underwent a rapid and dramatic process of neoliberal reform in the 1980s and 1990s, with the sale of state assets, the removal of tariffs and subsidies, reductions in welfare, the introduction of market rates in social housing, and the rise of cultures of accountability and performativity in public institutions. Education, particularly in the tertiary sector, was reconceived as something to be traded in an international marketplace, with private benefits but little value as a public good (Peters & Roberts, 1999). The idea was to enhance choice for students, minimising bureaucracy while maximising competition between tertiary education providers. Underpinning this shift in thinking was a conception of human beings as rational, self-interested, individual consumers (Olssen, 2001; Peters and Marshall, 1996). The move to a modified version of Third Way politics (Giddens, 1998, 2000) in the New Zealand context from 1999 to 2008 rubbed off some of the harsher edges of neoliberalism, with the 'more market' mantra giving way to an emphasis on advancing the country as a knowledge society and economy. An attempt was made to create a 'shared vision' for tertiary education, with greater inclusiveness and support for Māori and Pasifika aspirations (Ministry of Education, 2002). In some respects, however, aspects of the neoliberal reform process – competition within and between institutions, and the commodification of knowledge – were pushed even further during this period (Roberts & Peters, 2008). This has been particularly evident in the move to a performance-based system for research funding and the growth of 'export education' as an industry.

These changes have influenced all academic lives in New Zealand. Philosophers of education can contribute significantly in identifying, explaining and critiquing the ontological, epistemological, and ethical assumptions underpinning neoliberal reforms. There is also much that we can do in setting these policy ideas in their broader intellectual and political contexts. But we must acknowledge that we too have been shaped by neoliberalism; our very survival as academics has often depended on a certain kind of adaptability. We have all been expected to 'perform', in the narrow sense demanded by managerialist regimes, and this has exacted its toll on us as we have tried to reconcile our ideals with the sometimes brutal realities of institutional politics. Neoliberalism has, despite its demonstrable failures (Apple, 2001; Best, 2020), endured as the dominant paradigm for policy reform across four decades. As an amalgamation of different ideas, it has demonstrated a certain elasticity, taking on new forms in specific contexts over the years. Managerialism has been less flexible but similarly notable for its longevity in changing the nature of institutional life. Managerialist practices remained in place during the 'Third Way' years in the New Zealand context, were reinforced even more strongly in the post-Third Way years of 2008–2017, and have continued largely unchanged under the current government.

As the years went by, institutional support at the University of Auckland for work in the social, philosophical and historical foundations of education, along with other areas such as adult education, declined. Many who were part of the CPSE group in 1995 and 1996 moved on to other positions within or beyond New Zealand, and most were not replaced. Meanwhile, my research continued to develop in new directions, with an emerging interest in the value of literature for philosophical and educational inquiry. This programme of reading and writing would grow to become a key research area in the years ahead. While there is a substantial body of philosophical work on literature, ethics and the emotions (e.g., Barrow, 2004; Carr, 2005; Gribble, 1983; Jollimore & Barrios, 2006; Novitz, 1987; Palmer, 1992; Solomon, 1986), much of this has focused primarily on *theorising* such connections. My principal concern has been to *demonstrate* what literature has to offer by taking selected novels and plays as examples for analysis. (For further discussion of this approach, see Roberts, 2008a, 2015b, 2022a.) This project builds on a tradition of ethical inquiry established by philosophers such as Cunningham (2001) and Nussbaum (1990, 1995), and educationists such as Katz (1997), Sichel (1992), and Siegel (1997), among others.

I have paid particular attention to fictional work by Fyodor Dostoevsky, Leo Tolstoy, Hermann Hesse, Albert Camus, and Iris Murdoch (see, for example, Roberts, 2008a, 2008b, 2010, 2012b, 2016, 2019c, 2021b; Roberts & Freeman-Moir, 2013; Roberts & Saeverot, 2018). In the case of Dostoevsky, I have found much that is helpful in both his shorter fiction (Dostoevsky, 1997, 2004) and the great novels of his maturity (Dostoevsky, 1991, 1993, 1994, 2001). With Tolstoy, it has been both his influential short story, 'The Death of Ivan Ilyich' (Tolstoy, 2009) and a non-fiction work, his *Confession* (Tolstoy, 1987). In considering what Hesse has to offer educationists, I have focused on *Siddhartha* (Hesse, 2000a), *The Journey to the East* (Hesse, 1956), and *The Glass Bead Game* (Hesse, 2000b). With Camus, it has been a combination of novels, a short story, and a play (Camus, 1958, 1991, 1996, 2000). I have also, in discussing philosophy, death and education (Roberts, 2020b), made reference to Camus' famous essay, *The Myth of Sisyphus* (Camus, 1991). Murdoch's *The Bell* (Murdoch, 2004) and *The Philosopher's Pupil* (Murdoch, 2000) have provided food for thought in considering questions of utopia and dystopia, and her chief philosophical work, *The Sovereignty of Good* (Murdoch, 2001) has allowed me to extend my understanding of the importance of attention in education, a notion also developed by Simone Weil. In offering papers on these authors at conferences and other

PHILOSOPHY OF EDUCATION AS A WAY OF LIFE 115

events, I have found lovers of literature in surprising places, with some very stimulating dialogues during and after my presentations.

With literary works having occupied such a special place in my life for so long, I was at first reluctant to treat them in a new 'academic' way. For many years, when time from other duties permitted, I read novels by the above mentioned writers, together with works by Homer, Virgil, Cervantes, Shakespeare, George Eliot, Virginia Woolf, Franz Kafka, Janet Frame, Graham Greene, Umberto Eco, Ben Okri, Milan Kundera, Patricia Grace, and Margaret Atwood, among others, but I did so as a kind of 'private' ethical and literary education. My wife and I would sometimes read the same books and discuss them in the evenings. Reading was an important part of our home life, and 'home' was meant, to some degree, to be separate from 'work'. I was concerned that subjecting the novels I loved to more formal philosophical analysis would destroy my enjoyment of them. These fears proved to be unfounded. I have found myself appreciating these works in new ways. The discipline required to construct a tight, well-structured argument in response to a novel or play has sharpened the questions I wanted to ask of texts. It has opened up the range of sources I now include on student reading lists. It has allowed me to draw connections that hitherto had been obscured between different thinkers. It has taught me that the barriers between different genres of writing are not as rigid as we are sometimes led to believe. Indeed, many of the novelists I find most engaging, most helpful when addressing educational and ethical questions, are also fine philosophers. Iris Murdoch is an excellent example of this (see Roberts & Freeman-Moir, 2013), but it is also possible to read Dostoevsky, Camus, and many others in this light, even if they did not claim the label 'philosopher' for themselves (compare, Ford, 2004; Hanna, 1958; Scanlan, 2002).

Research never occurs in a 'pure' space; instead, it often must be conducted under institutional conditions that are always complex and often draining. Sabbatical leave for a semester in 2004, with visits to colleagues in Canada and the presentation of a number of talks at different universities, provided a brief, partial intellectual oasis. When I returned from leave, however, the CPSE group faced some of its sternest challenges. Some excellent scholars and committed teachers remained but by the middle of the first decade in the new century it had become increasingly difficult to maintain viable programmes of study at undergraduate and Masters levels in key areas. The amalgamation of the University of Auckland and the Auckland College of Education provided something of a boost to this dire state of affairs, with the opportunity, from 2006, to join kindred spirits at what became known as the Epsom Campus. The sociological study of education in particular was considerably strengthened by the merger, and there were also promising signs for philosophical and critical policy work. Interest in the study of philosophy of education at doctoral level was high, despite the paucity of university positions in the field. I had come to realise that this was the part of my job I valued most: the quiet, patient, in-depth work one undertakes in supervising serious research students. With the amalgamation and the relatively senior position I had in my new School I was able to take this commitment further, serving in various research mentoring roles with colleagues. This was just the preparation I needed for my next move.

In April 2008 I relocated to Christchurch to take up a chair at the University of Canterbury. I was appointed to offer research leadership, and I welcomed the opportunity to build on the supervision and mentoring work I'd undertaken in Auckland. My wife and I could also see benefits in giving our children a chance to experience the beauty and splendour of New Zealand's South Island for a few years before they reached adulthood. I settled into my new role quickly, and within 12 months I was chairing the College of Education Research Commit-tee, writing research plans, developing mentoring schemes, organising semi-nars and symposia, and receiving a steady stream of inquiries about doctoral supervision. For the first six months of 2009 I also served, in an acting capacity, as Associate Dean (Postgraduate) in the College. As it turned out, demand for philosophical and policy research among doctoral candidates in Education was as high in Christchurch as it had been in Auckland, and it didn't take long before I found myself in the unfortunate position of having to turn away prospective students. As had been the case in Auckland, limits had to be set on the number of doctoral candidates one could accept, given that most of us also had to teach at undergraduate and Master's levels. For the last dozen years or more, I have often worked with 8–10 doctoral students (plus Master's thesis students) at any one time. While high by New Zealand university standards, such numbers are not altogether unusual. Thankfully, my undergraduate teaching load at the Uni-versity of Canterbury has, for the most part, been very reasonable.

Canterbury has also been very good to me in many other ways, providing opportunities to spend time at the University of Oxford (as a Canterbury Fel-low based in the Education Department in 2010 and 2016) and the University of Cambridge (as a Rutherford Visiting Scholar at Trinity College in 2012). I loved the architecture, the sense of history, and the cultures of academic excel-lence at both of these extraordinary institutions. Invitations to give Keynotes and other academic addresses have taken me to a number of other parts of the globe, and my College has been supportive of these contributions. Throughout this time, I have been heavily involved with the Philosophy of Education Soci-ety of Australasia (PESA), serving on the Executive for nine years, three of them as President. As noted in Chapter 5, after some difficult years in the late 1990s and early 2000s, PESA has over the last 15 or more years gone from strength

PHILOSOPHY OF EDUCATION AS A WAY OF LIFE   117

to strength. Boosted by the success of the Society's journal, *Educational Philosophy and Theory*, edited by Michael Peters, PESA has provided a welcoming environment for younger and newer scholars as well as 'old hands'. As an organisation, its reach now extends well beyond Australia and New Zealand, with members and conference participants from many different parts of Asia as well as North America and Europe. In my role as President of the Society, I was keen to continue building our links with other philosophy of education groups across the world. Differences must be recognised and respected, but there is also much that we have in common. Struggles to retain positions in our field, and to play an active part in teacher education, are shared by many. Similarly, while there is no one best way of responding to dominant trends in educational thinking – e.g., the obsession with measurement, performance, and accountability (Biesta, 2010; Roberts & Peters, 2008) – such developments are of serious concern to a good number of educational philosophers. Solidarity and support have never been more needed than they are now.

My time at Canterbury has also been shaped significantly by something else we never could have expected when we moved here as a family in early 2008: the devastating earthquakes of September 2010 and February 2011, with literally thousands of aftershocks between and after these events. More than 180 people were killed in the February 2011 quake. Many houses and city buildings were damaged or destroyed. The University of Canterbury is located in an area that fared better than most in the quakes. Still, several key buildings on campus have been put out of action (including a five-storey tower block on the former College of Education site, now demolished), and with a decline in student enrolments following the quakes there were widespread redundancies. Most Christchurch residents have been affected in one way or another by these events, and there will be years of rebuilding ahead. But the city has proven itself to be remarkably resilient, with businesses relocating and reinventing themselves in novel ways, communities supporting each other, and new programmes of research and teaching on earthquake-related topics and themes emerging in the university. The quakes, together with later tragic events such as the March 2019 terror attack on mosques in the city, have shaped the way many at the University of Canterbury think about themselves as academics and as citizens of Christchurch; these events have prompted us to ask searching ethical questions of ourselves and to reassess personal priorities.

Partly as a response to the earthquakes and their consequences but also for other reasons, I found myself writing more directly on the nature of despair and its significance for educationists (Roberts, 2013a, 2013b, 2016; Roberts & Saeverot, 2018). This has led into further work on death (Roberts, 2020b, 2021b), another area often treated as a 'no-go' zone for academics. Addressing these themes has allowed me to see with greater clarity why and how I work as a philosopher of education. A number of other theorists have addressed questions relating to suffering, despair, and the tragic sense of education (e.g., Arcilla, 1992; Boler, 2004; Burbules, 1997; Chen, 2011; Liston, 2000), and my current work is intended to complement these studies. Drawing on literary figures such as Dostoevsky (1997, 2004), as well as Kierkegaard (1985, 1987, 1988, 1989), Schopenhauer (1969), Unamuno (1972), Weil (1997, 2001), Beauvoir (1948), and other more contemporary philosophers (e.g., Dienstag, 2006), I have argued that despair need not be conceived as something we must always seek to avoid or overcome. Despair, understood in a certain way, can be seen as a defining feature of human life. Education, in developing our capacity for reflective and critical thought, can enhance our awareness of injustices, intensify our frustrations in not being able to adequately understand and change ourselves and the world, and thereby heighten our sense of despair. But it can also enable us to work with despair in more fruitful ways. Through education, we can come to more deeply understand the suffering experienced by others and place our own troubles in broader perspective. Acknowledging the central role that despair plays in many lives need not mean the abandonment of hope or happiness. To the contrary, it is precisely in situations of despair that hope comes into its own, gaining renewed significance and meaning. Accepting that despair can be part of a well lived human life, without endorsing it or promoting it, can allow one to more deeply appreciate the joy in small things. It can help us to see qualities in ourselves and others that may previously have been obscured. It can permit us to value what we have, while holding on to our dreams, and foster greater openness to the unknown and the unexpected.

4   Conclusion

My own journey as a philosopher of education has taken me into 'unknown and unexpected' territory, and I have as many questions now as I had when growing up in Auckland. There is inevitably much that remains hidden in any account of this kind. A reader will often be left in the dark on many matters of detail relating to family or working life. Inner struggles and tensions can never be fully conveyed through the written word, even if we were inclined to reveal such things. Lives are frequently characterised not by a smooth, upward path of development, with a succession of high points in a glorious career, but by unevenness and messiness. A retrospective examination of a philosophical journey can gloss over, or ignore entirely, traumatic events, sustained periods of difficulty, and chronic pain. It can place before readers the masks we hold up to ourselves, our frailties and burdens too much to bear. These silences

PHILOSOPHY OF EDUCATION AS A WAY OF LIFE 119

notwithstanding, there is also much that can be gained from a deliberate attempt to examine one's work in a more autobiographical manner than is usually warranted. Among other benefits that may accrue from such an exercise is the encouragement it offers in trying to see links between different parts of a life – different research programmes, different activities, different ways of tackling problems. When I look back now on the path I've taken, I can see that, despite some detours, it has been largely constructed on a set of questions and concerns that troubled me from childhood.

I found my way to Freire not just because Colin Lankshear pointed me there but also because in Freirean theory and practice questions about education, ethics and the meaning of life are to the fore. Freire offers not a perfect recipe or method for educational success but an ethic of humanisation that can serve us well in a variety of personal and professional situations. From Freire, Lao Tzu, Simone Weil, and many others we can learn the importance of humility, equanimity, patience, commitment, and care, whether this is in a classroom with 30 students, a meeting with colleagues, or an e-mail discussion. Freire and Weil, together with Kierkegaard, Dostoevsky, Nietzsche, Unamuno, Camus, Beauvoir, and Murdoch, may have had their faults, but they faced up more resolutely and honestly than most to the despair, and the joys, of human life. Many of the thinkers to whom I feel most closely connected, and I include here literary figures as well as philosophers and educationists, lived in some way 'on the edge'. They had questions that couldn't be easily answered. They had doubts and uncertainties. They were restless and uncomfortable. They suffered greatly but they were also able to appreciate the beauty and goodness that exists all around us. The destructiveness of neoliberalism as a doctrine for economic and social development also plays its part in creating a sense of despair, and a need for ongoing work in building better worlds. Philosophy of education helps us on our way in addressing these problems. As a field, it is under constant threat of dismissal within teaching programmes, but it has refused to be extinguished. As a profession, it promises neither wealth nor unending happiness. As a mode of being, philosophy of education makes life harder, not easier, but it is all the more important for that. I for one am looking forward to continuing this difficult journey.

Acknowledgement

This chapter is an updated version of Roberts, P. (2014). An accident waiting to happen: Reflections on a philosophical life in Education. In L. J. Waks (Ed.), *Leaders in philosophy of education* (Vol. 2, pp. 211–229). Sense Publishers. With permission from Brill (https://brill.com).

References

Althusser, L. (1971). *Lenin and philosophy and other essays* (B. Brewster, Trans.). New Left Books.

Andersen, B. (2009). PESA: A memoir. *Educational Philosophy and Theory, 41*(7), 742–744.

Apple, M. (2001). Comparing neo-liberal projects and inequality in education. *Comparative Education, 37*(4), 409–423.

Apple, M. W. (1999). *Power, meaning, and identity: Essays in critical educational studies.* Peter Lang.

Arcilla, R. V. (1992). Tragic absolutism in education. *Educational Theory, 42*(4), 473–481.

Arcilla, R. V. (2002). Why aren't philosophers and educators speaking to each other? *Educational Theory, 52*(1), 1–11.

Ardern, J. (2019, January 22). New Zealand hopes the world will follow its wellness-based policies. *Financial Times.* https://www.ft.com/content/6b425632-18c1-11e9-b191-175523b59d1d

Argenton, G. (2017). Mind the gaps: Controversies about algorithms, learning and trendy knowledge. *E-Learning and Digital Media, 14*(3), 183–197.

Aronowitz, S. (2012). Paulo Freire's radical democratic humanism: The fetish of method. In M. Nikolakaki (Ed.), *Critical pedagogy in the new dark ages: Challenges and possibilities* (pp. 257–274). Peter Lang.

Arnold, K. (1995). The body in the virtual library: Rethinking scholarly communication. *Journal of Electronic Publishing,* 1.

Ashcroft, C. (2005). Performance based research funding: A mechanism to allocate funds or a tool for academic promotion? *New Zealand Journal of Educational Studies, 40*(1), 113–129.

Astle, D. (1991, December 12). High prices from Elsevier. *Newsletter on Serials Pricing Issues,* NS 15.

Attaran, M., Stark, J., & Stotler, D. (2018). Opportunities and challenges for big data analytics in US higher education: A conceptual model for implementation. *Industry and Higher Education, 32*(3), 169–182.

Baggaley, J. (2013). MOOC rampant. *Distance Education, 34*(3), 368–378.

Balestra, C., Boarini, R., & Tosetto, E. (2018). What matters most to people? Evidence from the OECD Better Life Index users' responses. *Social Indicators Research, 136,* 907–930.

Ball, S. J. (2003). The teacher's soul and the terrors of performativity. *Journal of Education Policy, 18*(2), 215–228.

Barrow, R. (2004). Language and character. *Arts and Humanities in Higher Education, 3,* 267–279.

Bauman, Z. (1988). Is there a postmodern sociology? *Theory, Culture and Society, 5*, 217–237.

Bauman, Z. (1993). The fall of the legislator. In T. Docherty (Ed.), *Postmodernism: A reader* (pp. 128–140). Harvester Wheatsheaf.

Beauvoir, S. de (1948). *The ethics of ambiguity* (B. Frechtman, Trans.). Citadel Press.

Benade, L. (2012). *From technicians to teachers: Ethical teaching in the context of globalised education reform.* Continuum.

Bence, V., & Oppenheim, C. (2005). The evolution of the UK's Research Assessment Exercise: Publications, performance and perceptions. *Journal of Educational Administration and History, 37*(2), 137–155.

Ben-Porath, S., & Shahar, T. H. B. (2017). Big data and education: Ethical and moral challenges. *Theory and Research in Education, 15*(3), 243–248.

Bernard, G. W. (2000). History and research assessment exercises. *Oxford Review of Education, 26*(1), 95–106.

Best, J. (2020). The quiet failures of early neoliberalism: From rational expectations to Keynesianism in reverse. *Review of International Studies, 46*(5), 594–612.

Biebricher, T. (2018). *The political theory of neoliberalism.* Stanford University Press.

Biesta, G. (2010). *Good education in an age of measurement.* Paradigm.

Billsberry, J. (2013). MOOCs: Fad or revolution? *Journal of Management Education, 37*(6), 739–746.

Binkley, S. (2011). Happiness, positive psychology and the program of neoliberal governmentality. *Subjectivity, 4*, 371–394.

Björk, B., Welling, P., Laakso, M., Majlender, P., Hedlund, T., & Gudnason, G. (2010). Open access to the scientific journal literature: Situation 2009. *PloS One, 5*(5), 1–9.

Blackmore, J. (2001). Universities in crisis? Knowledge economies, emancipatory pedagogies, and the critical intellectual. *Educational Theory, 51*(3), 353–371.

Boler, M. (2004). Teaching for hope: The ethics of shattering world views. In D. Liston & J. Garrison (Eds.), *Teaching, learning, and loving: Reclaiming passion in educational practice.* RoutledgeFalmer.

Bottrell, D., & Manathunga, C. (Eds.). (2019). *Resisting neoliberalism in higher education.* Palgrave Macmillan.

Bourdieu, P. (1998). *Acts of resistance: Against the new myths of our time.* Polity Press.

Bourdieu, P., & Passeron, J. C. (1977). *Reproduction in education, society and culture.* Sage.

Bowles, S., & Gintis, H. (1976). *Schooling in capitalist America.* Basic Books.

Bruns, A. (2013). Faster than the speed of print: Reconciling 'big data' social media analysis and academic scholarship. *First Monday, 18*(10). http://dx.doi.org/10.5210/fm.v18i10.4879

Budapest Open Access Initiative. (2002). Declaration: 14 February, Budapest, Hungary. http://www.budapestopenaccessinitiative.org/read

REFERENCES

Bullen, E., Robb, S., & Kenway, J. (2004). 'Creative destruction': Knowledge economy policy and the future of the arts and humanities in the academy. *Journal of Education Policy, 19*(1), 3–22.

Burbules, N. C. (1997). Teaching and the tragic sense of education. In N. C. Burbules & D. Hansen (Eds.), *Teaching and its predicaments*. Westview Press.

Camus, A. (1958). The misunderstanding. In *Caligula and three other plays* (S. Gilbert, Trans.). Vintage Books.

Camus, A. (1991). The guest. In *Exile and the kingdom* (J. O'Brien, Trans.). Vintage International.

Camus, A. (1996). *The first man* (D. Hapgood, Trans.). Penguin.

Camus, A. (2000). *The fall* (J. O'Brien, Trans.). Penguin.

Carr, D. (2005). On the contribution of literature and the arts to the educational cultivation of moral virtue, feeling and emotion. *Journal of Moral Education, 34*, 137–151.

Carr, W. (2004). Philosophy and education. *Journal of Philosophy of Education, 38*(1), 55–73.

Carusi, F. T. (2017). Why bother teaching? Despairing the ethical through teaching that does not follow. *Studies in Philosophy and Education, 36*, 633–645.

Cavalletti, B., & Corsi, M. (2018). 'Beyond GDP' effects on national subjective well-being of OECD countries. *Social Indicators Research, 136*, 931–966.

Chen, R. H. (2011). Bearing and transcending suffering with nature and the world: A humanistic account. *Journal of Moral Education, 40*(2), 203–216.

Chen, R. H. (2016). Freire and a pedagogy of suffering: A moral ontology. In M. A. Peters (Ed.), *Encyclopedia of educational philosophy and theory*. Springer.

Cigman, R. (2014). Happiness rich and poor: Lessons from philosophy and literature. *Journal of Philosophy of Education, 48*(2), 308–322.

Cigman, R. (2012). We need to talk about well-being. *Research Papers in Education, 27*(4), 449–462.

Clark, J. (2011, December 1–4). *Does philosophy of education have a future?* [Conference session] Paper presented at the Philosophy of Education Society of Australasia annual conference, Auckland University of Technology.

Clark, J. (2006). Philosophy of education in today's world and tomorrow's: A view from 'down under'. *Paideusis, 15*(1), 21–30.

Clarke, R. (2007). The cost profiles of alternative approaches to journal publishing. *First Monday, 12*(12). http://dx.doi.org/10.5210/fm.v12i12.2048

Codd, J. (1993). Neo-liberal education policy and the ideology of choice. *Educational Philosophy and Theory, 24*(2), 31–48.

Codd, J. (2001). The Third Way for tertiary education policy: TEAC and beyond. *New Zealand Annual Review of Education, 10*, 31–57.

Committee for Economic Development (2009). *Harnessing openness to improve research, teaching and learning in higher education*. Committee for Economic Development.

Cope, W., & Kalantzis, M. (2009). Signs of epistemic disruption: Transformations in the knowledge system of the academic journal. *First Monday, 14*(4). http://dx.doi.org/10.5210/fm.v14i4.2309

Cope, B., & Kalantzis, M. (2015). Sources of evidence-of-learning: Learning and assessment in the era of big data. *Open Review of Educational Research, 2*(1), 194–217.

Cunningham, A. (2001). *The heart of what matters: The role for literature in moral philosophy.* University of California Press.

Curtis, B. (2008). The Performance-Based Research Fund: Research assessment and funding in New Zealand. *Globalisation, Societies and Education, 6*(2), 179–194.

Daniel, B. (2015). Big data and analytics in higher education: Opportunities and challenges. *British Journal of Educational Technology, 46*(5), 904–920.

Darder, A. (2002). *Reinventing Paulo Freire: A pedagogy of love.* Westview Press.

Darder, A., Torres, R. D., & Boltodano, M. (Eds.). (2017). *The critical pedagogy reader* (3rd ed.). Routledge.

Davies, W. (2016). The new neoliberalism. *New Left Review, 101*, 121–134.

Dawson, M. C. (2020). Rehumanising the university for an alternative future: Decolonisation, alternative epistemologies and cognitive justice. *Identities, 27*(1), 71–79.

Day, C. (1995). Economics of electronic publishing. *Journal of Electronic Publishing*, 1.

Dean, M. (2014). Rethinking neoliberalism. *Journal of Sociology, 50*(2), 150–162.

Dearden, R. F., Hirst, P. H., & Peters, R. S. (Eds.). (1972). *Education and the development of reason.* Routledge & Kegan Paul.

Deem, R., & Brehony, K. J. (2005). Management as ideology: The case of 'new managerialism' in higher education. *Oxford Review of Education, 31*(2), 217–235.

Deem, R., Hillyard, S., & Reed, M. (2007). *Knowledge, higher education, and the new managerialism: The changing management of UK universities.* Oxford University Press.

Dewey, J. (1966). *Democracy and education.* Free Press.

Dewey, J. (1997). *Experience and education.* Touchstone.

Dewey, J. (1910). *How we think.* Heath.

Dickens, C. (2003). *A tale of two cities.* Penguin.

Dienstag, J. F. (2006). *Pessimism: Philosophy, ethic, spirit.* Princeton University Press.

Dostoevsky, F. (1991). *The brothers Karamazov* (R. Pevear & L. Volokhonsky, Trans.). Vintage.

Dostoevsky, F. (1993). *Crime and punishment* (R. Pevear & L. Volokhonsky, Trans.). Vintage.

Dostoevsky, F. (1994). *Demons* (R. Pevear & L. Volokhonsky, Trans.). Vintage.

Dostoevsky, F. (1997). The dream of a ridiculous man. In F. Dostoevsky (Ed.), *The eternal husband and other stories* (R. Pevear & L. Volokhonsky, Trans.) (pp. 296–319). Bantam Books.

Dostoevsky, F. (2001). *The idiot* (R. Pevear & L. Volokhonsky, Trans.). Granta.

REFERENCES

Dostoevsky, F. (2004). *Notes from underground* (R. Pevear & L. Volokhonsky, Trans.). Everyman's Library.

Ecclestone, K. (2011). Well-being and education. In J. Arthur & A. Peterson (Eds.), *The Routledge companion to education* (pp. 302–313). Routledge.

Ecclestone, K., & Hayes, D. (2008). *The dangerous rise of therapeutic education*. Routledge.

Eichhorn, S., & Matkin, G. W. (2016). Massive open online courses, big data, and education research. *New Directions for Institutional Research, 167*, 27–40.

Elton, L. (2000). The UK Research Assessment Exercise: Unintended consequences. *Higher Education Quarterly, 54*(3), 274–283.

Elwick, A., & Cannizzaro, S. (2017). Happiness in higher education. *Higher Education Quarterly, 71*(2), 204–219.

Escobar, M., Fernandez, A. L., Guevara-Niebla, G., & Freire, P. (1994). *Paulo Freire on higher education: A dialogue at the National University of Mexico.* State University of New York Press.

Evans, S., & McIntyre, K. (2016). MOOCs in the humanities: Can they reach underprivileged students? *Convergence: The International Journal of Research into New Media Technologies, 22*(3), 313–323.

Evers, C. W. (2009). Remembering PESA: An intellectual journey. *Educational Philosophy and Theory, 41*(7), 788–793.

Ferguson, I. (2007). Neoliberalism, happiness and wellbeing. *International Socialism: A Quarterly Review of Socialist Theory, 117*, 1–16.

Fitzsimons, P., Peters, M., & Roberts, P. (1999). Economics and the educational policy process in New Zealand. *New Zealand Journal of Educational Studies, 34*(1), 35–44.

Flew, T. (2014). Six theories of neoliberalism. *Thesis Eleven, 122*(1), 49–71.

Ford, R. (2004). Critiquing desire: Philosophy, writing and terror. *Journal of Human Rights, 3*(1), 85–98.

Foucault, M. (1979). *Discipline and punish: The birth of the prison* (A. Sheridan, Trans.). Peregrine.

Foucault, M. (1980). *Power/knowledge: Selected interviews and other writings, 1972–1977* (C. Gordon, L. Marshall, J. Mepham & K. Soper, Trans; C. Gordon, Ed.). Harvester Press.

Fraser, J. W. (1997). Love and history in the work of Paulo Freire. In P. Freire, J. W. Fraser, D. Macedo, T. McKinnon & W. T. Stokes (Eds.), *Mentoring the mentor: A critical dialogue with Paulo Freire* (pp. 175–199). Peter Lang.

Freire, P. (1972a). *Pedagogy of the oppressed*. Penguin.

Freire, P. (1972b). *Cultural action for freedom*. Penguin.

Freire, P. (1976). *Education: The practice of freedom*. Writers and Readers.

Freire, P. (1978). *Pedagogy in process: The letters to Guinea-Bissau*. Writers and Readers.

Freire, P. (1985). *The politics of education*. MacMillan.

Freire, P. (1987). Letter to North-American teachers. In I. Shor (Ed.), *Freire for the Classroom* (pp. 211–214). Boynton/Cook.

Freire, P. (1993). *Pedagogy of the city*. Continuum.

Freire, P. (1994). *Pedagogy of hope*. Continuum.

Freire, P. (1996). *Letters to Cristina: Reflections on my life and work*. Routledge.

Freire, P. (1997a). *Pedagogy of the heart*. Continuum.

Freire, P. (1997b). A response. In P. Freire, J. W. Fraser, D. Macedo, T. McKinnon & W. T. Stokes (Eds.), *Mentoring the mentor: A critical dialogue with Paulo Freire* (pp. 303–329). Peter Lang.

Freire, P. (1998a). *Teachers as cultural workers: Letters to those who dare teach*. Westview Press.

Freire, P. (1998b). *Pedagogy of freedom: Ethics, democracy, and civic courage*. Rowman & Littlefield.

Freire, P. (1998c). *Politics and education*. UCLA Latin American Center Publications.

Freire, P. (2004). *Pedagogy of indignation*. Paradigm Publishers.

Freire, P. (2007). *Daring to dream*. Paradigm Publishers.

Freire, P., & Faundez, A. (1989). *Learning to question: A pedagogy of liberation*. World Council of Churches.

Freire, P., Freire, A. M. A., & de Oliviera, W. F. (2014). *Pedagogy of solidarity*. Left Coast Press.

Freire, P., & Macedo, D. (1987). *Literacy: Reading the word and the world*. Routledge.

Freire, P., & Macedo, D. (1993). A dialogue with Paulo Freire. In P. McLaren & P. Leonard (Eds.), *Paulo Freire: A critical encounter* (pp. 169–176). Routledge.

Freire, P., & Macedo, D. (1995). A dialogue: Culture, language, and race. *Harvard Educational Review, 65*(3), 377–402.

Freire, P., & Shor, I. (1987). *A pedagogy for liberation*. MacMillan.

Fromm, E. (1942). *The fear of freedom*. Routledge & Kegan Paul.

Gibbs, P. (2015). Happiness and education: Troubling students for their own contentment. *Time and Society, 24*(1), 54–70.

Gibbs, P. (2017). Should contentment be a key aim in higher education? *Educational Philosophy and Theory, 49*(3), 242–252.

Gibbs, P., & Dean, A. (2014). Troubling the notion of satisfied students. *Higher Education Quarterly, 68*(4), 416–431.

Giddens, A. (1998). *The Third Way: The renewal of social democracy*. Polity Press.

Giddens, A. (2000). *The Third Way and its critics*. Polity Press.

Gietzen, G. (2010). Jean-Francois Lyotard and the question of disciplinary legitimacy. *Policy Futures in Education, 8*(2), 166–176.

Gilbert, J. (2005). Catching the knowledge wave? 'Knowledge society' and the future of public education. In J. Codd & K. Sullivan (Eds.), *Education policy directions in Aotearoa New Zealand* (pp. 53–70). Dunmore Press.

REFERENCES

Giroux, H. A. (1983). *Theory and resistance in education: A pedagogy for the opposition.* Bergin & Garvey.

Giroux, H. A. (1988). *Teachers as intellectuals: Toward a critical pedagogy of learning.* Bergin & Garvey.

Giroux, H. A. (1997). *Pedagogy and the politics of hope: Theory, culture, and schooling – A critical reader.* Westview Press.

Giroux, H. A. (2002). Neoliberalism, corporate culture, and the promise of higher education: The University as a democratic public sphere. *Harvard Educational Review, 72*(4), 424–463.

Giroux, H. A. (2005). The terror of neoliberalism: Rethinking the significance of cultural politics. *College Literature, 32*(1), 1–19.

Giroux, H. A. (2006). *America on the edge: Henry Giroux on politics, culture, and education.* Palgrave Macmillan.

Giroux, H. A. (2008). *Against the terror of neoliberalism: Politics beyond the age of greed.* Paradigm Publishers.

Giroux, H. A. (2011a, November 7). Beyond the limits of neoliberal higher education: Global youth resistance and the American/British divide. Posted by the Campaign for the Public University. http://publicuniversity.org.uk/2011/11/07/beyond-the-limits-of-neoliberal-higher-education-global-youth-resistance-and-the-americanbritish-divide/

Giroux, H. A. (2011b, December 19). Why faculty should join Occupy Movement protesters on college campuses. *Truthout.* http://www.truth-out.org/why-faculty-should-join-occupy-movement-protesters-college-campuses/1324328832

Giroux, H. A. (2019). Neoliberalism and the weaponising of language and education. *Race and Class, 61*(1), 26–45.

Goldsmith, P. (2017a, July 26). Government's response to the Productivity Commission inquiry into *New models of tertiary education.* Office of the Minister for Tertiary Education, Skills and Employment. Document prepared for the Cabinet Economic Growth and Infrastructure Committee.

Goldsmith, P. (2017b, July 27). *Response to the Productivity Commission report on tertiary education.* Speech.

Greene, M. (1973). *Teacher as stranger.* Wadsworth.

Greenwood, C. (1993). Publish or perish: The ethics of publishing in peer-reviewed journals. *Media Information Australia, 68*, 29–35.

Greyson, D., Vezina, K., Morrison, H., Taylor, D., & Black, C. (2009). University supports for open access: A Canadian national survey. *Canadian Journal of Education, 39*(3), 1–32.

Gribble, J. (1983). *Literary education: A revaluation.* Cambridge University Press.

Grugel, J., & Riggirozzi, P. (2012). Post neoliberalism: Rebuilding and reclaiming the state in Latin America. *Development and Change, 43*(1), 1–21.

Guardia, L., Maina, M., & Sangra, A. (2013). MOOC design principles: A pedagogical approach from the learner's perspective. *eLearning Papers, 33*, 1–5.

Guédon, J-C (2009). Open access: An old tradition and a new technology. *Canadian Journal of Education, 39*(3), i-v.

Guilherme, A., & de Freitas, A. L. S. (2017). 'Happiness education': A pedagogical-political commitment. *Policy Futures in Education, 15*(1), 6–19.

Gurría, A. (2019, July 8). *The economy of well-being.* Prepared remarks from the OECD Secretary-General for a European OECD Council meeting, Brussels.

Hadot, P. (1995). *Philosophy as a way of life.* (M. Chase, Trans.). Blackwell.

Hall, S., Massey, D., & Rustin, M. (2013). After neoliberalism: Analysing the present. *Soundings, 53*, 8–22.

Hammer, R., & Kellner, D. (Eds.). (2009). *Media/cultural studies: Critical approaches.* Peter Lang.

Hanna, T. (1958). *The thought and art of Albert Camus.* Henry Regnery.

Harnad, S. (1991). Post-Gutenberg galaxy: The fourth revolution in the means of production of knowledge. *Public-Access Computer Systems Review, 2*(1), 39–53.

Harnad, S. (1995). Electronic scholarly publication: Quo vadis. *Serials Review, 21*(1), 70–72.

Harnad, S. (1996). Implementing peer review on the Net: Scientific quality control in scholarly electronic journals. In R. P. Peek & G. B. Newby (Eds.), *Scholarly publishing: The electronic frontier* (pp. 103–118). MIT Press.

Harnad, S. (1997). The paper house of cards (and why it's taking so long to collapse). *Ariadne, 8.* http://www.ariadne.ac.uk/issue8/harnad/

Harnad, S., & Brody, T. (2004). Comparing the impact of Open Access (OA) vs. non-OA articles in the same journals. *D-Lib Magazine, 10*(6).

Harris, K. (1979). *Education and knowledge.* Routledge & Kegan Paul.

Harris, K. (1982). *Teachers and classes.* Routledge & Kegan Paul.

Harris, K. (2009). PESA and me. *Educational Philosophy and Theory, 41*(7), 745–751.

Harvey, D. (2005). *A brief history of neoliberalism.* Oxford University Press.

Harvie, D. (2000). Alienation, class and enclosure in UK universities. *Capital and Class, 71*, 103–132.

Haynes, B. (2009). Philosophy of Education Society of Australasia: The official record. *Educational Philosophy and Theory, 41*(7), 738–741.

Heidegger, M. (1996). *Being and time* (J. Stambaugh, Trans.). State University of New York Press.

Heidegger, M. (1997). The question concerning technology. In *The question concerning technology and other essays* (W. Lovitt, Trans.). Harper and Row.

Hellström, T., & Raman, S. (2001). The commodification of knowledge about knowledge: Knowledge management and the reification of epistemology. *Social Epistemology, 15*(3), 139–154,

REFERENCES

Hesse, H. (1956). *The journey to the east* (H. Rosner, Trans.). The Noonday Press.

Hesse, H. (2000). *The glass bead game* (R. Winston & C. Winston, Trans.). Vintage.

Hill, B. V. (2009). Seeking understanding by which to educate. *Educational Philosophy and Theory, 41*(7), 761–764.

Hirst, P. H. (1974). *Knowledge and the curriculum.* Routledge & Kegan Paul.

Hirst, P. H., & Peters, R. S. (1970). *The logic of education.* Routledge & Kegan Paul.

Hogan, P. (2006). Education as a discipline of thought and action: A memorial to John Wilson. *Oxford Review of Education, 32*(2), 253–264.

Holloway, J., & Brass, J. (2018). Making accountable teachers: The terrors and pleasures of performativity. *Journal of Education Policy, 33*(3), 361–382.

Holmwood, J. (2014). From social rights to the market: Neoliberalism and the knowledge economy. *International Journal of Lifelong Education, 33*(1), 62–76.

hooks, b. (1982). *Ain't I a woman: Black women and feminism.* Pluto Press.

hooks, b. (1984). *Feminist theory from margin to center.* South End Press.

hooks, b. (1989). *Talking back: Thinking feminist, thinking Black.* South End Press.

hooks, b. (1990). *Yearning: Race, gender, and cultural politics.* South End Press.

hooks, b. (1992). *Black looks: Race and representation.* South End Press.

hooks, b. (1993). *Sisters of the yam: Black women and self-recovery.* South End Press.

hooks, b. (1993b). bell hooks speaking about Paulo Freire – The man, the work. In P. McLaren & P. Leonard (Eds.), *Paulo Freire: A critical encounter* (pp. 146–154). Routledge.

hooks, b. (1994a). *Teaching to transgress: Education as a practice of freedom.* Routledge.

hooks, b. (1994b). *Outlaw culture: Resisting representations.* Routledge.

hooks, b. (1995). *Killing rage: Ending racism.* Holt.

hooks, b. (1996). *Reel to reel: Race, sex, and class at the movies.* Routledge.

hooks, b. (2000). *Where we stand: Class matters.* Routledge.

hooks, b. (2003). *Teaching community: A pedagogy of hope.* Routledge.

hooks, b. (2004). *We real cool: Black men and masculinity.* Routledge.

hooks, b. (2009). *Belonging: A culture of place.* Routledge.

hooks, b. (2010). *Teaching critical thinking: Practical wisdom.* Routledge.

Horton, M., & Freire, P. (1990). *We make the road by walking: Conversations on education and social change.* Temple University Press.

Howarth, J. P., D'Alessandro, S., Johnson, L., & White, L. (2016). Learner motivation for MOOC registration and the role of MOOCs as a university 'taster'. *International Journal of Lifelong Education, 35*(1), 74–85.

Iiyoshi, T., & Kumar, M. S. V. (Eds.). (2008). *Opening up education.* The MIT Press.

Illich, I. (1971). *Deschooling society.* Penguin.

Irwin, J. (2018). Radicalising philosophy of education – The case of Jean-Francois Lyotard. *Educational Philosophy and Theory, 50*(6–7), 692–701.

Jackson, L., & Bingham, C. (2018). Reconsidering happiness in the context of social justice education. *Interchange: A Quarterly Review of Education, 49*, 217–229.

Jardine, D. W., McCaffrey, G., & Gilham, C. (2014). The pedagogy of suffering: Four fragments. *Paideusis, 21*(2), 5–13.

Jessop, B. (2002). Liberalism, neoliberalism, and urban governance: A state-theoretical perspective. *Antipode*, 452–472.

Jollimore, T., & Barrios, S. (2006). Creating cosmopolitans: The case for literature. *Studies in Philosophy and Education, 25*, 263–283.

Jona, K., & Naidu, S. (2014). MOOCs: Emerging research. *Distance Education, 35*(2), 141–144.

Kahn, R. (2010). *Critical pedagogy, ecoliteracy, and planetary crisis*. Peter Lang.

Katz, M. (1997). On becoming a teacher: May Sarton's *The small room. Philosophy of Education, 1997*. Philosophy of Education Society.

Kellner, D. (1995). *Media culture: Cultural studies, identity, and politics between the modern and the postmodern*. Routledge.

Kellner, D. (2003). *Media spectacle*. Routledge.

Kellner, D., Lewis, T., Pierce, C., & Cho, K. D. (Eds.). (2009). *Marcuse's challenge to education*. Rowman & Littlefield.

Kenny, J. (2017). Academic work and performativity. *Higher education, 74*(5), 897–913.

Kierkegaard, S. (1985). *Philosophical fragments* (H. V. Hong & E. H. Hong, Trans.). Princeton University Press.

Kierkegaard, S. (1987). *Either/or*, 2 vols. (H. V. Hong & E. H. Hong, Trans.). Princeton University Press.

Kierkegaard, S. (1988). *Stages on life's way* (H. V. Hong & E. H. Hong, Trans.). Princeton University Press.

Kierkegaard, S. (1989). *The sickness unto death* (A. Hannay, Trans.). Penguin.

Kincheloe, J. L. (2007). Critical pedagogy in the twenty-first century: Evolution for survival. In P. McLaren & J. Kincheloe (Eds.), *Critical pedagogy: Where are we now?* (pp. 9–42). Peter Lang.

Kincheloe, J. L. (2008a). *Critical pedagogy primer* (2nd ed.). Peter Lang.

Kincheloe, J. L. (2008b). *Knowledge and critical pedagogy*. Springer.

King's College London and Digital Science (2015). *The nature, scale and beneficiaries of research impact: An initial analysis of Research Excellence Framework (REF) 2014 impact case studies*. HEFCE.

Kirylo, J. D. (2011). *Paulo Freire: The man from Recife*. Peter Lang.

Kirylo, J. D. (Ed.). (2013). *A critical pedagogy of resistance*. Sense Publishers.

Klikauer, T. (2015). What is managerialism? *Critical Sociology, 41*(7–8), 1103–1119.

Koller, H-C. (2003). Bildung and radical plurality: Towards a redefinition of Bildung with reference to J-F. Lyotard. *Educational Philosophy and Theory, 35*(2), 155–165.

Kumar, R. (Ed.). (2016). *Neoliberalism, critical pedagogy and education*. Routledge.

REFERENCES

Lange, J. (2015). Rise of the digitized public intellectual: Death of the professor in the network neutral Internet age. *Interchange: A Quarterly Review of Education, 46*, 95–112.

Lao Tzu (1963). *Tao Te Ching* (D. C. Lau, Trans.) Penguin.

Lather, P. (2020). Updata: Post-neoliberalism. *Qualitative Inquiry, 26*(7), 768–770.

Law, W-W. (2019). *Politics, managerialism, and university governance: Lessons from Hong Kong under China's rule since 1997*. Springer.

Layard, R. (2005). *Happiness: Lessons from a new science*. Penguin.

Leistyna, P. (2007). Neoliberal non-sense. In P. McLaren & J. Kincheloe (Eds.), *Critical pedagogy: Where are we now?* (pp. 97–123). Peter Lang.

Levinas, E. (1969). *Totality and infinity* (A. Lingis, Trans.). Duquesne University Press.

Levinas, E. (1998). *Otherwise than being or beyond essence* (A. Lingis, Trans.). Duquesne University Press.

Lewis, T. E. (2012). *The aesthetics of education: Theatre, curiosity, and politics in the work of Jacques Rancière and Paulo Freire*. Continuum.

Lewkowicz, J. (2015). Post-neoliberalism: Lessons from South America. *openDemocracyUK*, 9 February.

Liston, D. P. (2000). Love and despair in teaching. *Educational Theory, 50*(1), 81–102.

Liu, K. (2014). *Conscientization and the cultivation of conscience*. Peter Lang.

Locke, K. (2015). Performativity, performance and education. *Educational Philosophy and Theory, 49*(3), 247–259.

Longstaff, E. (2017). How MOOCs can empower learners: A comparison of provider goals and user experiences. *Journal of Further and Higher Education, 41*(3), 314–327.

Lynch, K. (2015). Control by numbers: New managerialism and ranking in higher education. *Critical Studies in Education, 56*(2), 190–207.

Lyotard, J-F. (1984). *The postmodern condition: A report on knowledge* (G. Bennington & B. Massumi, Trans.). University of Minnesota Press.

Lyotard, J-F. (1988). *The differend: Phrases in dispute*. (G. V. D. Abbeele, Trans.). University of Minnesota Press.

Lyotard, J-F. (1993). *Political writings* (B. Readings & K. P. Geiman, Trans.). University of Minnesota Press.

Macedo, D. (1997). An anti-method pedagogy: A Freirian perspective. In P. Freire, J. W. Fraser, D. Macedo, T. McKinnon & W. T. Stokes (Eds.), *Mentoring the mentor: A critical dialogue with Paulo Freire* (pp. 1–9). Peter Lang.

Mack, M. (2014). *Philosophy and literature in times of crisis: Challenging our infatuation with numbers*. Bloomsbury.

Mackie, R. (1980). Contributions to the thought of Paulo Freire. In R. Mackie (Ed.), *Literacy and revolution: The pedagogy of Paulo Freire* (pp. 93–119). Pluto Press.

Marshall, J. (1987). *Positivism or pragmatism: Philosophy of education in New Zealand*. New Zealand Association for Research in Education.

Marshall, J. (1996). The autonomous chooser and 'reforms' in education. *Studies in Philosophy and Education, 15*, 89–96.

Marshall, J. (1999). Performativity: Lyotard and Foucault through Searle and Austin. *Studies in Philosophy and Education, 18*, 309–317.

Marx, K. (1964). *Economic and philosophical manuscripts of 1844* (M. Milligan, Trans., D. Struik, Ed.). International Publishers.

Marx, K. (1976). *Capital*, vol. 1 (B. Fowkes, Trans., E. Mandel, Ed.). Penguin.

Marx, K., & Engels, F. (1972). *The Communist manifesto*. In R. C. Tucker (Ed.), *The Marx-Engels reader*. Norton.

May, C. (2010). Openness in academic publication: The question of trust, authority and reliability. *Prometheus, 28*(1), 91–94.

Mayo, P. (1999). *Gramsci, Freire and adult education: Possibilities for transformative action*. Zed Books.

Mayo, P. (2004). *Liberating praxis: Paulo Freire's legacy for radical education and politics*. Praeger.

McKenzie, J. (2001). *Perform or else: From discipline to performance*. Routledge.

McKnight, D. (2010). Critical pedagogy and despair: A move toward Kierkegaard's passionate inwardness. In E. Malewski (Ed.), *Curriculum studies handbook: The next moment* (pp. 500–516). Routledge.

McLaren, P. (1989). *Life in schools: An introduction to critical pedagogy in the foundations of education*. Longman.

McLaren, P. (1997). *Revolutionary multiculturalism: Pedagogies of dissent for the new millennium*. Westview Press.

McLaren, P. (2000). *Che Guevara, Paulo Freire, and the pedagogy of revolution*. Rowman & Littlefield.

McLaren, P., & Kincheloe, J. (Eds.). (2007). *Critical pedagogy: Where are we now?* Peter Lang.

Middleton, S. (2005). Disciplining the subject: The impact of PBRF on education academics. *New Zealand Journal of Educational Studies, 40*(1), 131–156.

Mika, C. (2015). Counter-colonial and philosophical claims: An indigenous observation of Western philosophy. *Educational Philosophy and Theory, 47*(11), 1136–1142.

Mika, C., & Stewart, G. (2016). Māori in the kingdom of the gaze: Subjects or critics? *Educational Philosophy and Theory, 48*(3), 300–312.

Miller, A. (2008). A critique of positive psychology – or 'the new science of happiness'. *Journal of Philosophy of Education, 42*(3–4), 591–608.

Ministry of Education. (2002). *Tertiary education strategy, 2002/07*. Ministry of Education.

Ministry of Education. (2006). *Tertiary education strategy, 2007–12*. Ministry of Education (Office of the Associate Minister of Education – Tertiary Education).

Ministry of Education. (2009). *Tertiary education strategy, 2010–15*. Ministry of Education (Office of the Minister for Tertiary Education).

REFERENCES

133

Ministry of Education. (2020). *The Statement of National Education and Learning Priorities (NELP) and Tertiary Education Strategy (TES)*. Ministry of Education.

Mintz, A. (2013). 'Helping by hurting': The paradox of suffering in social justice education. *Theory and Research in Education, 11*(3), 215–230.

Morrison, H. (2013). Economics of scholarly communication in transition. *First Monday, 18*(6). http://dx.doi.org/10.5210/fm.v18i6.4370.

Morrow, R. A., & Torres, C. A. (2002). *Reading Freire and Habermas: Critical pedagogy and transformative social change*. Teachers College Press.

Murdoch, I. (1999). *Existentialists and mystics: Writings on philosophy and literature*. Penguin.

Murdoch, I. (2001). *The sovereignty of good*. Routledge.

New Zealand Government. (2014). *Tertiary education strategy, 2014–2019*. Ministry of Education and Ministry of Business, Innovation and Employment.

New Zealand Productivity Commission. (2016). *New models of tertiary education: Issues paper*. https://www.productivity.govt.nz/inquirycontent/tertiary-education

New Zealand Productivity Commission. (2017a) *New models of tertiary education: Final Report*. https://www.productivity.govt.nz/inquiry-content/tertiary-education

New Zealand Productivity Commission. (2017b). New models of tertiary education are coming, ready or not. Press release, March 21, 2017.

Nieto Ángel, M. C., Maciel Vahl, M., & Farrell, B. (2020). Critical pedagogy, dialogue and tolerance: A learning to disagree framework. In S. L. Macrine (Ed.), *Critical pedagogy in uncertain times: Hope and possibilities* (2nd ed., pp. 139–158). Palgrave Macmillan.

Nietzsche, F. (1966). *Beyond good and evil* (W. Kaufmann, Trans.). Vintage Books.

Nietzsche, F. (1967). *The birth of tragedy* and *The case of Wagner* (W. Kaufmann, Trans.). Vintage Books.

Nietzsche, F. (1968). *The will to power* (W. Kaufmann, Trans.; W. Kaufmann & R. J. Hollingdale, Eds.). Vintage Books.

Nietzsche, F. (1974). *The gay science* (W. Kaufmann, Trans.). Vintage Books.

Nietzsche, F. (1976a). *Thus spoke Zarathustra*. In W. Kaufmann (Ed.), *The portable Nietzsche* (pp. 103–439). Penguin.

Nietzsche, F. (1976b). *Twilight of the idols*. In W. Kaufmann (Ed.), *The portable Nietzsche* (pp. 463–563). Penguin.

Nietzsche, F. (1976c). *The AntiChrist*. In W. Kaufmann (Ed.), *The portable Nietzsche* (pp. 565–656). Penguin.

Nietzsche, F. (1989). *On the genealogy of morals* and *Ecce homo* (W. Kaufmann, Trans.). Vintage Books.

Nietzsche, F. (1990). *Beyond good and evil* (R. J. Hollingdale, Trans.). Penguin.

Nietzsche, F. (1996). *Human, all too human* (R. J. Hollingdale, Trans.). Cambridge University Press.

Nietzsche, F. (1997). *Daybreak: Thoughts on the prejudices of morality* (R. J. Hollingdale, Trans.; M. Clark & B. Leiter, Eds.). Cambridge University Press.

Nietzsche, F. (1997). *Untimely meditations* (R. J. Hollingdale, Trans., D. Breazeale, Ed.). Cambridge University Press.

Nikolakaki, M. (Ed.). (2012). *Critical pedagogy in the new dark ages: Challenges and possibilities.* Peter Lang.

Novitz, D. (1987). *Knowledge, fiction and imagination.* Temple University Press.

Nussbaum, M. (1990). *Love's knowledge: Essays on philosophy and literature.* Oxford University Press.

Nussbaum, M. (1995). *Poetic justice: The literary imagination and public life.* Beacon Press.

Nussbaum, M. (2010). *Not for profit: Why democracy needs the humanities.* Princeton University Press.

Nuyen, A. T. (1992). Lyotard on the death of the professor. *Educational Theory, 42*(1), 25–37.

Odlyzko, A. M. (1994). Tragic loss or good riddance? The impending demise of traditional scholarly journals. *Surfaces, 4.*

Odlyzko, A. M. (1997). The economics of electronic journals. *First Monday, 2*(8). http://dx.doi.org/10.5210/fm.v2i8.542

OECD. (2013). *OECD guidelines on measuring subjective well-being.* OECD Publishing. http://dx.doi.org/10.1787/9789264191655-en

OECD. (2015). *The innovation imperative: Contributing to productivity, growth and well-being.* OECD Publishing. http://dx.doi.org/10.1787/9789264239814-en

OECD. (2017). *How's life? 2017: Measuring well-being.* OECD Publishing. https://doi.org/10.1787/how_life-2017-en

OECD Better Life Initiative. (2017). *How's life in New Zealand?* OECD Statistics and Data Directorate.

OECD Better Life Initiative. (2019). *Measuring well-being and progress.* OECD Statistics and Data Directorate.

Okerson, A. (1991a). The electronic journal: What, whence, and when? *Public-Access Computer Systems Review, 2*(1), 5–24.

Okerson, A. (1991b). Back to academia? The case for American universities to publish their own research. *Logos, 2*(2), 106–112.

Okerson, A. (1996). University libraries and scholarly communication. In R. P. Peek & G. B. Newby (Eds.), *Scholarly publishing: The electronic frontier* (pp. 181–199). MIT Press.

O'Loughlin, M. (2009). PESA then and now: Recollections and congratulations. *Educational Philosophy and Theory, 41*(7), 804–807.

Olssen, M. (2001). *The neo-liberal appropriation of tertiary education policy in New Zealand: Accountability, research and academic freedom.* New Zealand Association for Research in Education.

REFERENCES

Olssen, M. (2004). Neoliberalism, globalisation, democracy: Challenges for education. *Globalisation, Societies and Education, 2*(2), 231–275.

Olssen, M., & Peters, M. A. (2005). Neoliberalism, higher education and the knowledge economy: From the free market to knowledge capitalism. *Journal of Education Policy, 20*(3), 313–345.

Ozga, J. (1998). The entrepreneurial researcher: Re-formations of identity in the research marketplace. *International Studies in Sociology of Education, 8*(2), 143–153.

Ozolins, J. (2003). Suffering: Valuable or just useless pain? *Sophia, 42*(2), 53–77.

Palmer, F. (1992). *Literature and moral understanding: A philosophical essay on ethics, aesthetics, education, and culture.* Clarendon Press.

PBRF Review Panel. (2020). *E koekoe te tūī, e ketekete te kākā, e kūkū te kererū: Toward the Tertiary Research Excellence Evaluation (TREE).* The Report of the PBRF Review Panel. Ministry of Education.

Peck, J. (2010). *Constructions of neoliberal reason.* Oxford University Press.

Performance-Based Research Fund Working Group. (2002). *Investing in excellence: The report of the Performance-Based Research Fund Working Group.* Ministry of Education and Transition Tertiary Education Commission.

Peters, M. (1989). Techo-science, rationality, and the university: Lyotard on the 'postmodern condition'. *Educational Theory, 39*(2), 93–105.

Peters, M. (1994). 'Performance', the future of the university and 'post-industrial' society. *Educational Philosophy and Theory, 26*(1), 1–22.

Peters, M. (Ed.). (1995). *Education and the postmodern condition.* Bergin & Garvey.

Peters, M. (1997). Wittgenstein and post-analytic philosophy of education: Rorty or Lyotard? *Educational Philosophy and Theory, 29*(2), 1–32.

Peters, M. A. (2006). Lyotard, nihilism and education. *Studies in Philosophy and Education, 25,* 303–314.

Peters, M. A. (2009a). Self-editorializing: PESA and *Educational Philosophy and Theory,* after twenty-five years. *Educational Philosophy and Theory, 41*(7), 801–803.

Peters, M. A. (2009b). Editorial. *Educational Philosophy and Theory, 41*(7), 735–737.

Peters, M. A. (2011). *Neoliberalism and after? Education, social policy and the crisis of capitalism.* Peter Lang.

Peters, M. A. (2012). Algorithmic capitalism and educational futures: Informationalism and the Googlization of knowledge. *Truthout,* 4 May.

Peters, M., & Besley, T. (2006). *Building knowledge cultures.* Rowman & Littlefield.

Peters, M., Lankshear, C., & Olssen, M. (Eds.). (2003). *Critical theory and the human condition: Founders and praxis.* Peter Lang.

Peters, M., & Marshall, J. (1996). *Individualism and community: Education and social policy in the postmodern condition.* Falmer Press.

Peters, M., & Roberts, P. (Eds.). (1998). *Virtual technologies and tertiary education.* Dunmore Press.

Peters, M., & Roberts, P. (1999). *University futures and the politics of reform in New Zealand.* Dunmore Press.

Peters, M. A., & Roberts, P. (2011). *The virtues of openness: Education, science, and scholarship in the digital age.* Paradigm Publishers.

Peters, R. S. (1970). *Ethics and education.* Allen & Unwin.

Peters, R. S. (1973). *Authority, responsibility and education.* George Allen & Unwin.

Petrilli, M. J. (2018). Big data transforms education research. *Education Next*, Winter, 86–87.

Priem, J., & Hemminger, B. (2010). Scientometrics 2.0: New metrics of scholarly impact on the social Web. *First Monday, 15*(7). http://dx.doi.org/10.5210/fm.v15i7.2874.

Prinsloo, P. (2017). Fleeing from Frankenstein's monster and meeting Kafka on the way: Algorithmic decision-making in higher education. *E-Learning and Digital Media, 14*(3), 138–163.

Pyati, A. (2007). A critical theory of open access: Libraries and electronic publishing. *First Monday, 12*(10). http://dx.doi.org/10.5210/fm.v12i10.1970.

Rappleye, J., Komatsu, H., Uchida, Y., Krys, K., & Markus, H. (2020). 'Better policies for better lives'?: Constructive critique of the OECD's (mis)measure of student well-being. *Journal of Education Policy, 35*(2), 258–282.

Reveley, J. (2016). Neoliberal meditations: How mindfulness training medicalizes education and responsibilizes young people. *Policy Futures in Education, 14*(4), 497–511.

Roberts, P. (1995a). Defining literacy: Paradise, nightmare or red herring? *British Journal of Educational Studies, 43*(4), 412–432.

Roberts, P. (1995b). Literacy studies: A review of the literature, with signposts for future research. *New Zealand Journal of Educational Studies, 30*(2), 189–214.

Roberts, P. (1996a). Critical literacy, breadth of perspective, and universities: Applying insights from Freire. *Studies in Higher Education, 21*(2), 149–163.

Roberts, P. (1996b). Defending Freirean intervention. *Educational Theory, 46*(3), 335–352.

Roberts, P. (1997a). A critique of the NZQA policy reforms. In M. Olssen & K. Morris Matthews (Eds.), *Education policy in New Zealand: The 1990s and beyond* (pp. 16–189). Dunmore Press.

Roberts, P. (1997b). The consequences and value of literacy: A critical reappraisal. *Journal of Educational Thought, 31*(1), 45–67.

Roberts, P. (1997c). Political correctness, great books and the university curriculum. In M. Peters (Ed.), *Cultural politics and the university* (pp. 103–134). Dunmore Press.

Roberts, P. (1997d). Literacies in cyberspace. *SET: Research Information for Teachers* (Special issue on language and literacy), July, item 3.

Roberts, P. (1998a). Rereading Lyotard: Knowledge, commodification and higher education. *Electronic Journal of Sociology, 3*(3).

REFERENCES 137

Roberts, P. (1998b). The politics of curriculum reform in New Zealand. *Curriculum Studies, 6*(1), 29–46.

Roberts, P. (1999a). Scholarly publishing, peer review and the Internet. *First Monday, 4*(4). http://firstmonday.org/ojs/index.php/fm/article/view/661/576.

Roberts, P. (1999b). A dilemma for critical educators? *Journal of Moral Education, 28*(1), 19–30.

Roberts, P. (1999c). The future of the university: Reflections from New Zealand. *International Review of Education, 45*(1), 65–85.

Roberts, P. (Ed.). (1999d). *Paulo Freire, politics and pedagogy: Reflections from Aotearoa-New Zealand.* Dunmore Press.

Roberts, P. (2000). *Education, literacy, and humanization: Exploring the work of Paulo Freire.* Bergin & Garvey.

Roberts, P. (2001). Nietzsche and the limits of academic life. In M. Peters, J. Marshall & P. Smeyers (Eds.), *Nietzsche's legacy for education: Past and present values* (pp. 125–137). Bergin & Garvey.

Roberts, P. (2003a). Epistemology, ethics and education: Addressing dilemmas of difference in the work of Paulo Freire. *Studies in Philosophy and Education, 22*(2), 157–173.

Roberts, P. (2003b). Contemporary curriculum research in New Zealand. In W. Pinar (Ed.), *The international handbook of curriculum research* (pp. 495–516). Lawrence Erlbaum.

Roberts, P. (2004). Neoliberalism, knowledge and inclusiveness. *Policy Futures in Education, 2*(2), 350–364.

Roberts, P. (2005). Tertiary education, knowledge and neoliberalism. In J. Codd & K. Sullivan (Eds.), *Education policy directions in Aotearoa New Zealand* (pp. 39–51). Thomson/Dunmore Press.

Roberts, P. (2006). Performativity, measurement and research: A critique of Performance-Based Research Funding in New Zealand. In J. Ozga, T. Popkewitz & T. Seddon (Eds.), *World yearbook of education 2006: Education research and policy* (pp. 185–199). Routledge.

Roberts, P. (2007a). Neoliberalism, performativity and research. *International Review of Education, 53*(4), 349–365.

Roberts, P. (2007b). Intellectuals, tertiary education and questions of difference. *Educational Philosophy and Theory, 39*(5), 480–493.

Roberts, P. (2008a). Bridging literary and philosophical genres: Judgement, reflection and education in Camus' *The Fall. Educational Philosophy and Theory, 40*(7), 873–887.

Roberts, P. (2008b). Teaching, learning and ethical dilemmas: Lessons from Albert Camus. *Cambridge Journal of Education, 38*(4), 529–542.

Roberts, P. (2009). Hope in troubled times? PESA and the future of philosophy of education. *Educational Philosophy and Theory, 41*(7), 811–813.

Roberts, P. (2010). *Paulo Freire in the 21st century: Education, dialogue and transformation*. Paradigm Publishers.

Roberts, P. (2011). Attention, asceticism and grace: Simone Weil and higher education. *Arts and Humanities in Higher Education, 10*(3), 315–328.

Roberts, P. (2012a). Scholars, philosophers or performers? The politics of research in contemporary universities. In R. Openshaw & J. Clark, J. (Eds.), *Critic and conscience: Essays in memory of John Codd and Roy Nash* (pp. 87–104). New Zealand Council for Educational Research.

Roberts, P. (2012b). *From West to East and back again: An educational reading of Hermann Hesse's later work*. Sense Publishers.

Roberts, P. (2013a). Happiness, despair and education. *Studies in Philosophy and Education, 32*(5), 463–475.

Roberts, P. (2013b). Education, faith, and despair: Wrestling with Kierkegaard. *Philosophy of Education Yearbook 2013* (pp. 277–285). Philosophy of Education Society.

Roberts, P. (2013c). Simone Weil: Education, spirituality and political commitment. In J. Kirylo (Ed.), *A critical pedagogy of resistance: 34 pedagogues we need to know* (pp. 129–132). Sense Publishers.

Roberts, P. (2014). Tertiary education and critical citizenship. In J. E. Petrovic & A. M. Kuntz (Eds.), *Citizenship education around the world: Local contexts and global possibilities* (pp. 220–236). Routledge.

Roberts, P. (2015a). Paulo Freire and utopian education. *Review of Education, Pedagogy, and Cultural Studies, 37*(5), 376–392.

Roberts, P. (Ed.). (2015b). *Shifting focus: Strangers and strangeness in literature and education*. Routledge.

Roberts, P. (2016). *Happiness, hope, and despair: Rethinking the role of education*. Peter Lang.

Roberts, P. (2017a). Paulo Freire. In G. W. Noblit (Ed.), *Oxford research encyclopedia of education* (pp. 1–22). Oxford University Press. https://doi.org/10.1093/acrefore/9780190264093.013.10

Roberts, P. (2017b). Learning to live with doubt: Kierkegaard, Freire, and critical pedagogy. *Policy Futures in Education, 15*(7/8), 834–848.

Roberts, P. (2018). Theory as research: Philosophical work in education. In J. Quay, J. Bleazby, S. Stolz, M. Toscano & S. Webster (Eds.), *Theory and philosophy in education research: Methodological dialogues* (pp. 23–35). Routledge.

Roberts, P. (2019a). Philosophy of education. In A. Kamp (Ed.), *Education studies in Aotearoa: Key disciplines and emerging directions* (pp. 25–46). NZCER.

Roberts, P. (2019b). Thesis supervision: A Freirean approach. In C. A. Torres (Ed.), *The Wiley handbook of Paulo Freire* (pp. 521–534). Wiley-Blackwell.

REFERENCES

Roberts, P. (2019c). Literature, learning and liberation: Teaching Hermann Hesse's *Siddhartha*. In D. Boscaljon & A. J. Levinovitz (Eds.), *Teaching religion and literature* (pp. 183–193). Routledge.

Roberts, P. (2020a). Less certain but no less committed: Paulo Freire and Simone de Beauvoir on ethics and education. In J. D. Kirylo (Ed.), *Reinventing pedagogy of the oppressed: Contemporary critical perspectives* (pp. 135–146). Bloomsbury.

Roberts, P. (2020b). Philosophy, death, and education. In G. W. Noblit (Ed.), *Oxford research encyclopedia of education* (pp. 1–21). Oxford University Press. https://doi.org/10.1093/acrefore/9780190264093.013.1271

Roberts, P. (2021a). More than measurement: Education, uncertainty and existence. In P. Howard, T. Saevi, A. Foran & G. Biesta (Eds.), *Phenomenology and educational theory in conversation: Back to education itself.* Routledge.

Roberts, P. (2021b). Education, attention and transformation: Death and decreation in Tolstoy and Weil. *Studies in Philosophy and Education, 40*(6), 595–608.

Roberts, P. (2022a). Conscientization, compassion and madness: Freire, Barreto and the limits of education. *Review of Education, Pedagogy, and Cultural Studies, 44*(1), 4–24.

Roberts, P. (2022b). Truth, attention and higher education. In J. T. Ozolins (Ed.), *Education in an age of lies and fake news: Regaining a love of truth* (pp. 62–76). Routledge.

Roberts, P., & Freeman-Moir, J. (2013). *Better worlds: Education, art, and utopia.* Lexington Books.

Roberts, P., Gibbons, A., & Heraud, R. (2015). *Education, ethics and existence: Camus and the human condition.* Routledge.

Roberts, P., & Peters, M. A. (2008). *Neoliberalism, higher education and research.* Sense Publishers.

Roberts, P., & Saeverot, H. (2018). *Education and the limits of reason: Reading Dostoevsky, Tolstoy and Nabokov.* Routledge.

Rodriguez, N. M., & Villaverde, L. E. (Eds.). (2000). *Dismantling White privilege: Pedagogy, politics, and whiteness.* Peter Lang.

Rossatto, C. (2005). *Engaging Paulo Freire's pedagogy of possibility: From blind to transformative optimism.* Rowman & Littlefield.

Rozas Gomez, C. (2007). The possibility of justice: The work of Paulo Freire and difference. *Studies in Philosophy and Education, 26*, 561–570.

Scanlan, J. P. (2002). *Dostoevsky the thinker.* Cornell University Press.

Scheffler, I. (1960). *The language of education.* Charles C. Thomas.

Scheffler, I. (1973). *Reason and teaching.* Bobbs-Merrill.

Schopenhauer, A. (1969). *The world as will and representation*, 2 vols. (E. F. Payne, Trans.). Dover.

Schouten, G. (2017). On meeting students where they are: Teacher judgement and the use of data in higher education. *Theory and Research in Education, 15*(3), 321–338.

Schugurensky, D. (2012). *Paulo Freire*. Continuum.

Seddon, T., Bennett, D., Bobis, J., Bennett, S., Harrison, N., Shore, S., Smith, E., & Chan, P. (2012). *Living in a 2.2 world: ERA, capacity building and the topography of Australian educational research*. AARE-ACDE joint report.

Seligman, M. E. P. (2002). *Authentic happiness: Using the new positive psychology to realize your potential for lasting fulfillment*. Random House.

Sellar, S., & Lingard, B. (2014). The OECD and the expansion of PISA: New global modes of governance in education. *British Educational Research Journal, 40*(6), 917–936.

Senyshyn, Y. (2005). Rise of authoritarianism in higher education: A critical analysis of the Research Assessment Exercise in British universities. *Journal of Educational Thought, 39*(3), 229–244.

Sharp, R. (1980). *Knowledge, ideology and the politics of schooling: Towards a Marxist analysis of education*. Routledge & Kegan Paul.

Shaw, I., & Taplin, S. (2007). Happiness: A sociological critique of Layard. *Journal of Mental Health, 16*(3), 359–373.

Shepherd, S. (2018). Managerialism: An ideal type. *Studies in Higher Education, 43*(9), 1668–1678.

Shor, I. (1980). *Critical teaching and everyday life*. South End Press.

Shor, I. (1986). *Culture wars: School and society in the conservative restoration 1969–1984*. Routledge & Kegan Paul.

Shor, I. (Ed.). (1987). *Freire for the classroom*. Boynton/Cook.

Shor, I. (1992). *Empowering education*. Chicago University Press.

Shor, I. (1993). Education is politics: Paulo Freire's critical pedagogy. In P. McLaren & P. Leonard (Eds.), *Paulo Freire: A critical encounter* (pp. 25–35). Routledge.

Shor, I. (1996). *When students have power: Negotiating authority in a critical pedagogy*. University of Chicago Press.

Shor, I., & Pari, C. (Eds.). (1999). *Critical literacy in action: Writing, words, changing worlds*. Heinemann.

Shore, C., & Taitz, M. (2012). Who owns the university? Institutional autonomy and academic freedom in an age of knowledge capitalism. *Globalisation, Societies and Education, 10*(2), 201–219.

Sichel, B. A. (1992). Education and thought in Virginia Woolf's *To the lighthouse*. *Philosophy of Education 1992*. Philosophy of Education Society.

Siegel, H. (1997). *Rationality redeemed? Further dialogues on an educational ideal*. Routledge.

Siegel, H. (Ed.). (2009). *The Oxford handbook of philosophy of education*. Oxford University Press.

Sims, M. (2020). *Bullshit towers: Neoliberalism and managerialism in universities*. Peter Lang.

REFERENCES

Skea, C. (2017). Student satisfaction in higher education: Settling up and settling down. *Ethics and Education, 12*(3), 364–377.

Small, D. (2011). Neo-liberalism in crisis? Educational dimensions. *Policy Futures in Education, 9*(2), 258–266.

Smecher, A. (2008). The future of the electronic journal. *NeuroQuantology, 6*(1), 1–6.

Smith, R., & Jesson, J. (Eds.). (2005). *Punishing the discipline – the PBRF regime: Evaluating the position of Education – where to from here?* AUT and the University of Auckland.

Snijder, R. (2013). Measuring monographs: A quantitative method to assess scientific impact and societal relevance. *First Monday, 18*(5). http://dx.doi.org/10.5210/fm.v18i5.4250

Snook, I. (2009). Reflections on PESA: 1969–2009. *Educational Philosophy and Theory, 41*(7), 757–760.

Solomon, D. (2002). Talking past each other: Making sense of the debate over electronic publication. *First Monday, 7*(8). http://dx.doi.org/10.5210/fm.v7i8.978.

Solomon, R. C. (1986). Literacy and the education of the emotions. In S. de Castell, A. Luke & K. Egan (Eds.), *Literacy, society, and schooling: A reader* (pp. 37–58). Cambridge University Press.

Solomon, R. C. (1999). *The joy of philosophy.* Oxford University Press.

Spratt, J. (2017). *Wellbeing, equity and education: A critical analysis of policy discourses of wellbeing in schools.* Springer.

Springer, S. (2015). Postneoliberalism? *Review of Radical Political Economics, 47*(1), 5–17.

Standish, P. (2006). John Wilson's confused 'Perspectives on the philosophy of education'. *Oxford Review of Education, 32*(2), 265–279.

Steinberg, S. R. (2007). Preface. In P. McLaren & J. Kincheloe (Eds.), *Critical pedagogy: Where are we now?* (pp. ix–x). Peter Lang.

Stewart, G. (2018). From both sides of the indigenous-settler hyphen in Aotearoa New Zealand. *Educational Philosophy and Theory, 50*(8), 767–775.

Stewart, G., & Roberts, P. (2016). Philosophy of education, dialogue, and academic life in Aotearoa New Zealand. *Policy Futures in Education, 14*(2), 238–251.

Stiglitz, J. (1999). Knowledge as a global public good. In I. Kaul, I. Grunberg & M. Stern (Eds.), *Global public goods: International cooperation in the 21st century.* Oxford University Press.

Stolz, S. (2017). McIntyre, managerialism and universities. *Educational Philosophy and Theory, 49*(1), 38–46.

Stronach, I. (2007). On promoting rigour in educational research: The example of the RAE. *Journal of Education Policy, 22*(3), 343–352.

Suber, P. (2015). Open access overview. http://bit.ly/oa-overview

Suissa, J. (2008). Lessons from a new science? On teaching happiness in schools. *Journal of Philosophy of Education, 42*(3–4), 575–590.

Tan, C. (2018a). To be more fully human: Freire and Confucius. *Oxford Review of Education,* *44*(4), 370–382.

Tan, C. (2018b). Wither teacher-directed learning? Freirean and Confucian insights. *The Educational Forum, 82*(4): 461–474.

Taubes, G. (1996a, February 9). Science journals go wired. *Science, 271*(5250).

Taubes, G. (1996b, February 9). Speed of publication – stuck in first gear. *Science, 271*(5250).

Tertiary Education Advisory Commission. (2000). *Shaping a shared vision.* TEAC.

Tertiary Education Advisory Commission. (2001a). *Shaping the system.* TEAC.

Tertiary Education Advisory Commission. (2001b). *Shaping the strategy.* TEAC.

Tertiary Education Advisory Commission. (2001c). *Shaping the funding framework.* TEAC.

Tertiary Education Commission. (2004). *Evaluating research excellence: The 2003 assessment – overview and key findings.* Tertiary Education Commission.

Tertiary Education Commission. (2008). *Performance-Based Research Fund: Annual report 2007.* Tertiary Education Commission.

Tertiary Education Commission. (2013). *Performance-Based Research Fund: Evaluating research excellence – the 2012 assessment.* Tertiary Education Commission.

Thatcher, S. G. (1995). The crisis in scholarly communication. *Chronicle of Higher Education*, 3 March, B1-B2.

Thompson, G. (2017). Computer adaptive testing, big data and algorithmic approaches to education. *British Journal of Sociology of Education, 38*(6), 827–840.

Torres, C. A. (1994). Education and the archeology of consciousness: Freire and Hegel. *Educational Theory, 44*(4), 429–445.

Torres, C. A. (2009). *Education and neoliberal globalization.* Routledge.

Torres, C. A. (2014). *First Freire: Early writings in social justice education.* Teachers College Press.

UCSB Library Newsletter for Faculty. (1996). Why we buy fewer books and journals: The continuing crisis in scholarly communication, part II. University of California at Santa Barbara (Spring).

Unamuno, M. de (1972). *The tragic sense of life in men and nations* (A. Kerrigan, Trans.). Princeton University Press.

Usher, R. (2006). Lyotard's performance. *Studies in Philosophy and Education, 25*, 279–288.

Vaidhyanathan, S. (2009). The Googlization of universities. *The 2009 NEA Almanac of Higher Education*, 65–74.

Valauskas, E. (1997). Waiting for Thomas Kuhn: *First Monday* and the evolution of electronic journals. *First Monday, 2*(12). http://dx.doi.org/10.5210/fm.v2i12.567

Vandenberg, D. (2009). Thinking about education. *Educational Philosophy and Theory, 41*(7), 784–787.

REFERENCES

Vidovich, L., & Porter, P. (1999). Quality policy in Australian higher education of the 1990s: University perspectives. *Journal of Education Policy, 14*(6), 567–586.

Vokey, D. (2006). What are we doing when we are doing philosophy of education? *Paideusis, 15*(1), 45–55.

Waks, L. (2008). The analytical revolution in philosophy of education and its aftermath. In L. Waks (Ed.), *Leaders in philosophy of education: Intellectual self portraits* (pp. 1–13). Sense Publishers.

Walker, J. (2009). A PESA story. *Educational Philosophy and Theory, 41*(7), 752–756.

Wallowitz, L. (Ed.). (2008). *Critical literacy and resistance: Teaching for social justice across the secondary curriculum.* Peter Lang.

Wang, Y. (2017). Education policy research in the big data era: Methodological frontiers, misconceptions, and challenges. *Education Policy Analysis Archives, 25*(94), 1–21.

Ward, S. C. (2012). *Neoliberalism and the global restructuring of knowledge and education.* Routledge.

Watts, R. (2016). *Public universities, managerialism and the value of higher education.* Palgrave Macmillan.

Webster, R. S. (2017). Valuing and desiring purposes of education to transcend miseducative measurement practices. *Educational Philosophy and Theory, 49*(4), 331–346.

Webster, S. (2009). *Educating for meaningful lives through existential spirituality.* Sense Publishers.

Webster, S. (2016). The existential individual *alone* within Freire's socio-political solidarity. In M. A. Peters (Ed.), *Encyclopedia of educational philosophy and theory.* Springer.

Weil, S. (1997). *Gravity and grace* (A. Wills, Trans.). Bison Books.

Weil, S. (2001a). *Waiting for god* (E. Craufurd, Trans.). Perennial Classics.

Weston, M. (Ed.). (2001). *Philosophy, literature and the human good.* Routledge.

Whyte, D., & Wiegratz, J. (Eds.). (2016). *Neoliberalism and the moral economy of fraud.* Routledge.

Williamson, B. (2017). Who owns educational theory? Big data, algorithms and the expert power of education data science. *E-Learning and Digital Media, 14*(3), 105–122.

Williamson, B. (2018). The hidden architecture of higher education: Building a big data infrastructure for the 'smarter university'. *International Journal of Educational Technology in Higher Education, 15*(12), 1–26.

Willinsky, J. (2006). *The access principle: The case for open access to research and scholarship.* The MIT Press.

Willis, P. (1977). *Learning to labour: How working class kids get working class jobs.* Saxon House.

Wilsdon, J., Allen, L., & Belfiore, E. (2015). *The metric tide: Report of the independent review of the role of metrics in research assessment and management.* July 2015. DOI: 10.13140/RG.2.1.4929.1363.

Wilson, E. (2008). *Against happiness: In praise of melancholy*. Farrar, Straus & Giroux.

Wilson, J. (2003). Perspectives on the philosophy of education. *Oxford Review of Education, 29*(2), 279–303.

Wilson, J. A. (2017). *Neoliberalism*. Routledge.

Wink, J. (2011). *Critical pedagogy: Notes from the real world* (4th ed.). Pearson.

Wittgenstein, L. (1958). *Philosophical investigations* (G. E. M. Anscombe, Trans.). Basil Blackwell.

Wright, S., & Shore, C. (2018). *Death of the public university? Uncertain futures for higher education in the knowledge economy*. Berghahn Books.

Yeatman, A., & Costea, B. (Eds.). (2018). *The triumph of managerialism? New technologies of government and their implications for value*. Rowman & Littlefield.

Zembylas, M. (2000). Something 'paralogical' under the sun: Lyotard's *Postmodern Condition* and science education. *Educational Philosophy and Theory, 32*(2), 159–184.

Zembylas, M. (2020). (Un)happiness and social justice education: Ethical, political and pedagogic lessons. *Ethics and Education, 15*(1), 18–32.

Zepke, N. (2017). *Student engagement in neoliberal times: Theories and practices for learning and teaching in higher education*. Springer.

Index

big data 3, 8, 12, 19–21, 50

capitalism 1, 5, 40, 68, 69, 72, 79
choice 1, 5, 18, 27, 38, 55–57, 60, 62, 63, 71, 72, 79, 113
collegiality 4, 36, 57
commodification 1, 4, 10, 19, 23, 30, 37, 39, 40, 80, 113
competition 2, 4, 5, 7, 23–25, 27, 29, 37–39, 56–58, 62, 63, 69, 70, 72, 79, 113
consumption 7, 68, 69
Covid-19 27, 37, 65, 68, 79

dehumanisation 3, 5, 21, 52, 53, 93
dialogue 32, 41, 43, 48, 50, 90, 92, 95, 96, 102, 103, 110, 115
dystopia 4, 23, 30, 37–39, 114

efficiency 3, 5, 10, 12, 14, 17, 21, 23, 24, 29, 64, 79, 102

Freire, Paulo 3, 6, 21, 76, 90–97, 99–103, 106, 107, 109–112, 119

Hadot, Pierre 74, 80–83, 86, 87
happiness 5, 64, 66, 69–71, 82, 119
higher education 2, 4, 7–9, 11–16, 22, 25, 40, 42, 51, 78–80, 100, 111
hooks, bell 6, 89, 90, 97, 99–101, 103, 104
hope 6, 14, 33, 40, 66, 74, 78, 83, 88, 91, 93, 95, 101–103, 118
humanisation 20, 88, 92, 93, 95, 110, 119

impact 4, 7, 13, 20, 23, 24, 28, 30, 36, 40, 42, 45, 50–53, 67, 108
information 11, 12, 15, 17–19, 21, 24, 26, 30, 31, 33, 34, 49
intellectual 15, 23, 24, 30, 32, 34–39, 41, 42, 45, 50, 52, 71, 74, 76, 78, 88, 89, 91, 92, 102, 108, 112, 115
Internet 4, 5, 8, 17, 18, 23, 33, 34, 42, 43, 45, 49–51, 53

knowledge 1–4, 6–21, 23–25, 27, 29–37, 39, 41, 44, 45, 48, 52, 53, 57, 58, 62, 64, 67, 79, 80, 82, 84, 89, 92, 94–96, 100, 102, 109, 113

liberal arts 5, 8, 80
Lyotard, Jean-François 2–4, 7–15, 17–24, 26, 29–34, 37, 39, 52, 64, 112

managerialism 1, 2, 7, 57, 113
market 1, 2, 4, 10, 13, 14, 16, 17, 20, 24, 26, 27, 29, 38, 57, 60, 61, 63–65, 67, 69, 70, 79, 101, 102, 113
marketing 2, 8, 57, 58
measurement 7, 19–21, 31, 66, 70, 117
metrics 4, 35, 42, 51, 53
monitoring 2, 37, 61
MOOCS 13, 14

neoliberalism 1, 2, 7, 18, 32, 38, 39–41, 55, 78–80, 89, 90, 101, 102, 113, 119
New Zealand 2, 4, 5, 7, 16, 20, 23, 24, 26–30, 35, 37–40, 42, 45–47, 52, 55–61, 63–65, 67, 68, 72, 75–80, 105, 113, 114, 116, 117

OECD 5, 29, 56, 66–70, 72, 73
outputs 2, 4, 10, 20, 24, 28, 30–33, 38, 39, 41, 47, 49, 51, 52, 64, 66, 102

pedagogy 6, 40, 78, 88–91, 94, 98–100, 102–104, 106, 107, 109, 110
peer review 5, 20, 42, 43, 45, 46, 48–50
Performance-Based Research Fund 4, 13, 19, 20, 23, 24, 26, 28, 30, 35, 36, 42, 45–47, 53, 58
performativity 1–4, 6–21, 23–26, 30, 32, 39, 40, 42, 45, 48, 52, 64, 74, 80, 99, 113
philosophy as a way of life 82, 83
Philosophy of Education Society of Australasia 5, 74, 75, 116
Productivity Commission 5, 16, 55, 56, 58, 59, 61–65, 67, 68, 71–73

publishing   4, 19, 31, 38, 42–44, 47–51, 53

quality   16, 28–32, 36, 39, 46–49, 55, 60, 61, 63, 67

research   2, 4, 9, 13, 18, 20, 23–39, 41–48, 50–53, 58, 61, 64, 74, 78, 83, 109, 111, 113–117, 119

Shor, Ira   6, 89, 90, 97, 98, 103

technoscience   24

wellbeing   5, 55, 56, 64–73, 100, 107

Printed in the United States
by Baker & Taylor Publisher Services